KT-439-908

The Clandestine Cake Club

COOKBOOK

Lynn Hill

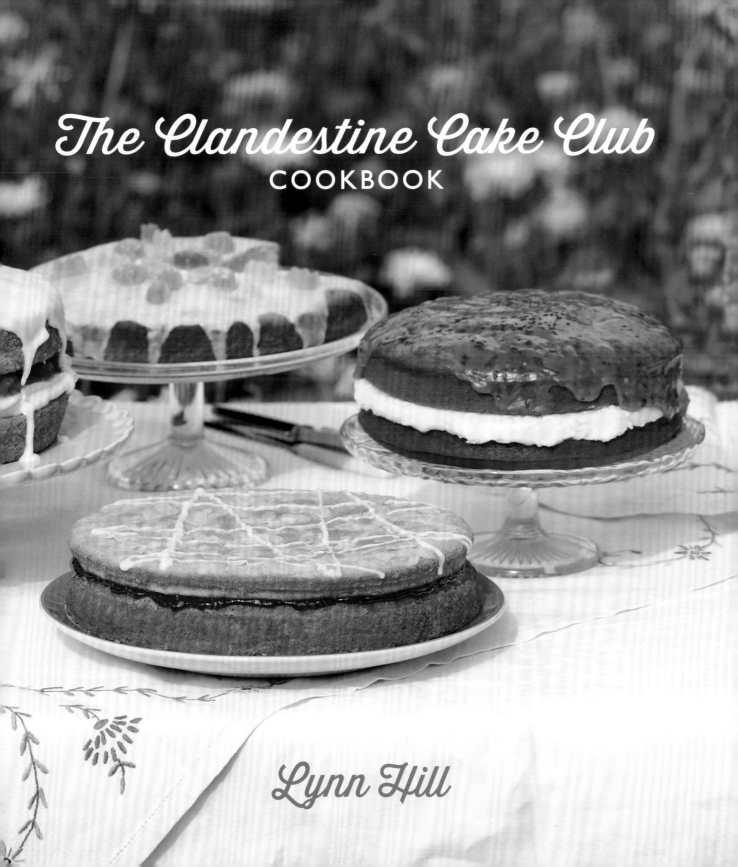

The Clandestine Cake Club
COOKBOOK

Lynn Hill

Dedication

This book is dedicated to home bakers everywhere,
who bake just for the sheer joy it brings them.

Contents

Bake, eat and talk about cake

A very simple concept, I thought. I was struck by the popularity of Supper Clubs, those secret dining societies that have been popping up all over the world. Wanting to put a twist on the idea, I started my own Secret Tea Room in my living room, which quickly became a big success. But never being one to stop at a good thing, I soon thought of a way to take it even further – why not have a secret gathering, completely about cake, where keen amateur bakers can all come together without a whiff of competition, each bringing a creative, delicious cake inspired by an imaginative event theme, to share with other like-minded cake-lovers? I thought how fun it would be to change the location each time, not letting anyone know where it would be taking place until the very last minute (that's the 'Clandestine' bit!). The only rules: no cupcakes (after all, a small cake's no good for sharing), no brownies, no cookies or pies.

a secret Leeds location for our first Clandestine Cake Club meeting. (An inflatable plastic parrot tied to the door ensured that everyone knew they had found the right place!) Our theme was Cake Cornucopia, which called for cakes with an abundance of flavours. Everyone got into the spirit and we shared some wonderful treats with such ingredients as orange, cinnamon, whisky, ginger, pink champagne and Earl Grey. Thus, the Clandestine Cake Club was born.

Subsequent events soon followed in Leeds … and then something amazing happened. Word of mouth and the excitement across social media sites meant that people beyond Leeds started to hear about our cakey events. People began asking me if I would hold an event near them. Since I couldn't be in all places at once (much as I try!), I encouraged people to set up their own Clandestine Cake Clubs (CCCs) and gave organisers simple rules and guidelines to follow. Well, who would have suspected how popular this would become?!

So, I put the word out on Twitter and on a winter afternoon in December 2010, ten happy bakers and seven irresistible cakes found themselves in

Word spread like wildfire, and before long we were featured by national media including the *Daily Mail*, *The One Show* and *The Alan Titchmarsh Show*. Every time we received major press coverage, so many people logged onto the CCC website that it crashed! Now, just two years since our first meeting, over 150 clubs have been established both here and abroad – with yet more being signed up every week.

Nobody is more amazed and impressed than I am by the incredible enthusiasm people have for secret baking! Not to mention the creativity and innovation shown by the club members. In addition to the amazing cakes themselves, Clandestine Cake Club events have been held in a variety of quirky places, including a castle, a cabin in the woods, an old-fashioned train station, an aeronautics club (where attendees could see and hear light aircraft and helicopters taking off in the background), in secret basements of vintage shops, in parks, village halls, coffee houses, espresso bars, restaurants and pubs, and of course in people's homes. Organisers have devised a whole host of fascinating and inspirational themes, such as 'Vintage Heaven', for which club members crafted shabby-chic-style cakes; 'A Novel Idea', which saw members bake cakes inspired by books, fairy tales or poems; and 'Baking with Beverages', which of course resulted in all kinds of naughty boozy treats.

The themes challenge bakers to be creative and imaginative, and often set members off on a personal quest for perfection; but as ever, the Clandestine Cake Club is not about competition.

That heart-warming community spirit and the incredible passion that members put into their baking were the inspiration behind this book. I put the call out for members to share their best recipes and was delighted when all manner of wonderful cake ideas began to pour in. It was so difficult to choose! But in the end we made our selections, and one thing all the cakes have in common is that none are beyond the reach of the home baker. So, in this book you'll not only find some of Cake Club's best recipes, but also tips and variations, information on frosting and icings and even advice on rescuing a dreaded cake wreck…!

I hope you will join me in enjoying these delicious cakes, and perhaps even attend a Cake Club event near you. Or maybe you want to set up your own Clandestine Cake Club? Find out how at **www.clandestinecakeclub.co.uk**.

Lynn Hill

Clandestine Cake Club members enjoy trying out unusual and inventive recipes, but we also know that sometimes the oldies are the best. In this chapter you'll find some of our favourite classic British and American cakes. One thing they all have in common is their deliciousness.

Aside from how moreish they are, these great recipes have earned their status as classics because they are generally quick and easy to make, and will often keep for several days. You just won't be able to stop yourself going back for another bite!

Classic Cakes

Banana Bread

LIZ LAIDLAW

Aromatic and easy, this is the perfect recipe for using up ripe bananas. The cake can be iced and decorated however you like – with buttercream (see page 248), a more decadent cream cheese frosting (as here), or with a quick glacé icing (see page 248) if you want to keep it simple. This cake will keep for up to five days if stored in an airtight tin and will become even more moist.

SERVES 12

100g butter, softened
200g golden caster sugar
2 eggs
250g plain flour, sifted
80ml whole milk
1 tsp lemon juice
1 tsp vanilla extract
3 large ripe bananas,
   well mashed
1 tsp bicarbonate of soda
pecan nuts, roughly chopped,
   to decorate (optional)

Cream Cheese Frosting (optional):

50g butter, softened
85g full-fat cream cheese
½ tsp vanilla extract
   (optional)
50g icing sugar

* Preheat the oven to 180°C/fan 160°C/gas mark 4. Grease and line a 900g loaf tin.

* Beat the butter and sugar using a wooden spoon or electric mixer until light and fluffy. Add the eggs one at a time, beating well after each addition, and adding a tablespoon of the flour with the final egg to help prevent curdling.

* Combine the milk and lemon juice in a jug, then add this liquid to the mixture along with the vanilla extract and banana. Mix well. Finally fold in the remaining flour and the bicarbonate of soda until thoroughly combined.

* Transfer the mixture to the tin, spreading it out evenly. Bake for 50 minutes–1 hour, until a skewer inserted into the centre comes out clean. Leave to cool in the tin for 10 minutes then turn out on to a wire rack to cool.

* For the frosting, beat the butter until smooth. Add the cream cheese and vanilla, if using, and mix until combined, then sift in the icing sugar and beat until light and fluffy. Spread over the top of the cooled cake and decorate with pecans if you wish. Store for up to five days in an airtight tin.

Scrumptious Sticky Toffee Cake

JANE EDGAR

This is a wonderful take on the classic British sticky toffee pudding. Don't worry if your cake sinks a little in the middle as this is actually a bonus – the creamy toffee sauce will gather in a delicious puddle. If you want to enjoy it like a pud, double up on the sauce recipe and serve with a big dollop of ice cream.

SERVES 8–10

225g dates, chopped
100ml milk
1 tsp bicarbonate of soda
115g butter, softened
170g soft light brown sugar
2 large eggs, beaten
170g self-raising flour
1 tsp vanilla extract

Toffee Sauce:
6 tbsp double cream
85g light muscovado sugar
30g butter

* Preheat the oven to 180°C/fan 160°C/gas mark 4. Grease and line a 20cm round cake tin.

* Put the dates into a small pan along with the milk and 100ml water. Bring to a simmer over a low heat and cook until all the liquid has been absorbed by the dates. Remove from the heat and leave to cool slightly, then add the bicarbonate of soda (it will fizz as you add it). Set aside to cool completely.

* Beat the butter and sugar using a wooden spoon or electric mixer until light and fluffy. Gradually add the eggs, beating well after each addition. If the mixture looks as if it's curdling, just add a tablespoon of the flour, then beat in the cooled date mixture and the vanilla extract. Finally sift in the rest of the flour and gently fold in until thoroughly combined.

* Spoon the mixture into the cake tin, spreading it evenly. Bake for 45–50 minutes, until firm to the touch. Leave to cool in the tin for a few minutes, then turn out on to a wire rack to cool completely.

* Meanwhile, make the toffee sauce. Put all the ingredients into a pan and gently heat until the sugar and butter are completely melted and the sauce has thickened slightly.

* Pour the sauce over the cooled cake and allow to run down the sides. It can help to turn the cake over first, as the underneath is often a bit neater and the sauce will run down the sides more easily, but you can leave it the right way up if you want extra sauce to gather in the dip in the middle of the cake (if there is one). Serve immediately with cream, ice cream, custard or just on its own.

Heavenly Carrot Cake

KIRSTY LLOYD

This classic moist cake has earned Kirsty a lot of fans at the florist's she works at, where you can often find cake and chrysanthemums side by side! This cake keeps amazingly well (unfrosted) and tastes even better after a day or two stored in an airtight tin. Just ice when you're ready to serve. With the aroma of spices, nuts and cinnamon, it's pretty heavenly!

SERVES 8–10

85g sultanas
juice of 1 large orange
85g wholemeal flour
85g self-raising flour
1 tsp mixed spice
1 tsp ground cinnamon
1 tsp bicarbonate of soda
½ tsp salt
170g soft light brown sugar
2 large eggs
125ml sunflower oil
170g carrots, peeled
  and grated
55g walnuts, chopped

Cream Cheese Frosting:
85g full-fat cream cheese
30g butter, softened
230g icing sugar
1 tsp vanilla extract

* Place the sultanas and orange juice in a small bowl and leave to soak overnight. Alternatively, if you don't have time for this, put the sultanas and juice into a small pan and place over a low heat for 2–3 minutes to encourage the sultanas to soak up the juice.

* Preheat the oven to 200°C/fan 180°C/gas mark 6. Grease and line a 20cm round, springform cake tin.

* Sift the flours, spices, bicarbonate of soda and salt into a large mixing bowl, then add the sugar and mix well.

* Whisk the eggs and combine them with the oil, then add the egg mixture to the dry ingredients and mix well. Fold in the carrot, walnuts and soaked sultanas until evenly distributed.

* Spoon the mixture into the tin and spread it out evenly. Bake for 40–45 minutes or until a skewer inserted into the centre comes out clean. Turn out on to a wire rack to cool completely.

* Meanwhile, make the cream cheese frosting. Whisk the cheese until soft and fluffy, then beat in the butter, icing sugar and vanilla extract until very smooth. Spread lashings of the frosting over the top of the cooled cake and serve.

Featherlight Cake

HELEN JONES

This butter-free sponge is light as a feather – its creator, Helen, suggests that 'air' ought to be listed as one of the ingredients! A very simple cake, made with just three basic ingredients, it can be sandwiched with your favourite filling and never fails to impress. The key to its success is remembering to fold in the flour as gently as possible, so that you don't beat out all that lovely air. See photo overleaf.

SERVES 8

4 eggs, separated
115g golden caster sugar
115g plain flour
1 tsp baking powder
icing sugar, to dust
  (optional)

Filling:
4 tbsp jam or lemon curd
150ml double cream

✳ Preheat the oven to 180°C/fan 160°C/gas mark 4. Grease and line two 18cm round sandwich tins.

✳ Whisk the egg whites until they form stiff peaks. Add the yolks one by one, whisking continuously. Gradually add the sugar and continue whisking until the mixture is very light and full of air and the whisk leaves a ribbon trail when lifted out.

✳ Sift in the flour and baking powder in two batches and fold in very gently using a metal spoon. Spoon the mixture into the tins and spread out evenly.

✳ Bake for 15–20 minutes, until the sponges are pale golden. Leave to cool in the tins for 10 minutes, then turn out on to a wire rack to cool completely.

✳ To fill the cake, spread the jam or lemon curd over one sponge. Whip the cream until it forms soft peaks, then carefully spoon over the jam. Top with the other sponge, then dust with icing sugar, if you wish.

Curious Victoria Sponge

ANDREW KITE

The ultimate classic cake has been made even better here, with a delicious boozy filling of berries, crème de cassis, orange extract and Cointreau. The result is a gorgeous treat that everyone will love. Any leftover berry filling can be kept in the fridge for a few days and is great served with your favourite ice cream.

SERVES 10–12

225g butter, at room temperature

225g caster sugar

4 eggs

225g self-raising flour

1 tsp vanilla extract

1 tsp orange extract

1 tsp Cointreau

1–2 tbsp milk, if required

1–2 tbsp good-quality berry jam, to fill

2 tbsp icing sugar, to dust

Berry Filling:

200g summer berries (such as blueberries, raspberries, strawberries)

1 tbsp caster sugar

1 tbsp crème de cassis

Cream Filling:

150ml double cream

1 tbsp Cointreau

2–3 drops of orange extract

For an alternative berry filling, try blackberries, loganberries and redcurrants. Fruit compote (available from supermarkets) also works well, but do add the crème de cassis to make it richer.

✳ Start by making the berry filling. Place the berries, sugar and crème de cassis in a small bowl and mix until the berries are thoroughly coated. Place in the fridge for about 2 hours (or overnight for a deeper flavour), stirring occasionally, to allow the flavours to combine.

✳ Preheat the oven to 190°C/fan 170°C/gas mark 5. Grease and line two 20cm round sandwich tins.

✳ Beat the butter and sugar using a wooden spoon or electric mixer until light and fluffy. Add the eggs one at a time, beating well after each addition, and adding a tablespoon of the flour with the final egg to help prevent curdling. Add the vanilla and orange extracts and the Cointreau.

✳ Slowly sift in the remaining flour and gently fold in until just combined. If the mixture looks a little stiff, add a tablespoon or so of milk to loosen it and reach a dropping consistency. Divide the mixture between the cake tins, spreading it evenly.

✳ Bake for 20–25 minutes or until a skewer inserted into each centre comes out clean and the tops spring back when gently pressed. Remove from the oven and allow to cool in the tins for 5 minutes, then turn out on to a wire rack to cool completely.

✳ For the cream filling, whip the cream with the Cointreau and a few drops of orange extract.

✳ To assemble, spread a layer of jam over one of the cooled sponges. Cover with the berry filling and spread evenly. Pipe or spoon the cream over the berries, then top with the other sponge. Dust with icing sugar.

PHOTO, FROM LEFT: CURIOUS VICTORIA SPONGE; FEATHERLIGHT CAKE

Caramel Cake

NELLY RITCHIE

Nelly baked this cake for her first-ever CCC event, proudly decorating it with caramel buttercream, a dusting of cocoa and glittery chocolate stars. But on her way to the event, disaster struck – the cake tin slipped from her hands and she was left with a brown, streaky cake wreck! Luckily, Nelly managed to rescue her cake with a generous layer of marshmallow fluff and a handful of mini marshmallows. Here she's given the recipe with the original buttercream coating, but feel free to use marshmallow fluff if you prefer!

SERVES 8

175g butter, softened
100g light muscovado sugar
200g canned caramel
1 x 9g sachet vanilla paste
  or 1 tsp vanilla extract
2 large eggs
175g plain flour
100g ground almonds
2 tsp baking powder
½ tsp ground cinnamon
pinch of ground cloves
pinch of ground ginger
chocolate curls, grated
  chocolate or glittery
  chocolate stars, to decorate

Caramel Buttercream:
45g butter, softened
100g canned caramel
300g icing sugar
pinch of cinnamon
1–2 tbsp milk

✳ Preheat the oven to 200°C/fan 180°C/gas mark 6. Grease and line two 18cm round sandwich tins.

✳ Beat the butter, sugar and caramel using a wooden spoon or electric mixer until light and fluffy, then add the vanilla paste or extract. Add the eggs one at a time, beating well after each addition, and adding a tablespoon of the flour with the final egg to help prevent curdling.

✳ Add the rest of the flour, almonds, baking powder and spices and continue beating until thoroughly combined. Divide the mixture between the tins, spreading it evenly.

✳ Bake the sponges for 25–35 minutes or until a skewer inserted into each centre comes out clean and the tops are springy to the touch. Leave to cool in the tins for a few minutes then turn out on to a wire rack to cool completely.

✳ Meanwhile, make the buttercream. Beat the butter and caramel until creamy, then sift in the icing sugar and cinnamon and beat until smooth. Add the milk, a little at a time, until the mixture has a spreading consistency.

✳ To assemble the cake, spread a layer of buttercream over one of the cooled sponges, then top with the other sponge and cover the top of the cake with the remaining buttercream. Decorate with chocolate curls, grated chocolate, or Nelly's preference – glittery chocolate stars!

Pineapple Upside-Down Cake

LYNN HILL

This retro cake dates back to 1920s America, when canned pineapple first appeared on shop shelves. My version has a lovely caramelised honey and pineapple topping. For a decadent touch, add a tablespoon of rum to the topping mixture. The cake can be kept in the fridge for a couple of days and is lovely served with whipped cream or custard.

SERVES 8

125g butter, softened
125g golden caster sugar
scraped seeds of 1 vanilla pod
2 eggs
125g self-raising flour
½ tsp baking powder
1 tbsp pineapple syrup
(from the can of rings
used for the topping)

Topping:
60g butter, softened
60g golden caster sugar
1 tbsp clear honey
4–5 canned pineapple rings
8 glacé cherries

* Preheat the oven to 190°C/fan 170°C/gas mark 5. Grease and line a 20cm round cake tin (not loose-bottomed).

* Start by making the topping. Beat the butter, sugar and honey until creamy and well combined, then spread evenly over the base of the tin.

* Place a pineapple ring in the centre of the mixture, then cut the remaining rings in half and arrange around the centre ring, cut-sides facing outwards but not touching the sides of the tin. Place a glacé cherry inside each pineapple hole.

* For the sponge, beat the butter and sugar using a wooden spoon or electric mixer until light and fluffy. Add the vanilla seeds, then add the eggs one at a time, beating well after each addition, and adding a tablespoon of the flour with the final egg to help prevent curdling.

* Fold in the remaining flour and the baking powder until thoroughly combined, then stir in the pineapple syrup. Spoon the mixture over the pineapple topping, spreading it evenly.

* Bake for 25 minutes or until a skewer inserted into the centre comes out clean. Leave to cool in the tin for a few minutes, then turn out on to a serving plate. Serve warm with a dollop of custard or cream, or just on its own.

Strawberry Shortcake

LYNN HILL

Strawberry shortcake is an American classic, but here I've given it a British twist by adapting a scone recipe from one of my mother's old recipe books. It's a perfect summer treat. As with scones, this is best eaten on the day it is made, but it will keep for a day if stored in the fridge. Be generous with the strawberries – why not serve some extra on the side to mop up any leftover cream?

SERVES 6–8

280g self-raising flour
1 tsp baking powder
50g caster sugar
85g butter, chilled, cut into small dice
1 large egg
100ml milk
½ tsp vanilla extract or the scraped seeds of 1 vanilla pod
caster sugar, to sprinkle

Filling:
350g strawberries, hulled and chopped in half
1 tbsp icing sugar
300ml whipping cream
½ tsp vanilla extract or the scraped seeds of 1 vanilla pod

✳ Preheat the oven to 200°C/fan 180°C/gas mark 6. Grease and line a 20cm round, loose-bottomed cake tin.

✳ Sift the flour and baking powder into a mixing bowl and stir in the sugar. Add the butter and use your fingertips to rub together until the mixture resembles breadcrumbs.

✳ Add the egg, milk and vanilla and mix until combined. Do not overwork. The mixture will be quite sticky but do not be tempted to add any more flour.

✳ Put the dough into the tin and use your fingers or the back of a spoon to gently press it to fit the tin. Bake for 20–25 minutes, until a skewer inserted into the centre comes out clean. Remove from the oven and turn out on to a wire rack to cool. Sprinkle over the caster sugar while warm.

✳ Make the filling by mashing half the strawberries with the icing sugar in a small bowl. Cover and leave in the fridge to marinate while the cake cools. Whip the cream until thick, then add the vanilla and whip until soft peaks form.

✳ Once the cake is completely cool, slice in half horizontally and spread the mashed strawberry mixture over the bottom layer, including any juices. Then place the remaining strawberries around the top edge of the cake, cover with the cream, then top with the other cake half. As with most scone mixtures, this is best eaten on the day it's made.

Mocha Marble Cake

CATHERINE PRATT

With swirls of cocoa and coffee, this marbled sponge contains wholemeal self-raising flour, which perhaps goes some way towards justifying all the indulgent buttercream that is used to fill and cover the cake! A slice of this is lovely served with a large mug of hot chocolate. See photo on page 24.

SERVES 8

170g butter, softened

170g caster sugar

3 large eggs

170g self-raising wholemeal flour (or regular self-raising flour if you prefer)

1 tbsp instant coffee granules, dissolved in 1 tbsp boiling water

1 tbsp cocoa powder, dissolved in 2 tbsp boiling water

Coffee Buttercream:

200g butter, softened

2 tbsp coffee granules, dissolved in 2–3 tbsp hot milk and left to cool

420g icing sugar

✳ Preheat the oven to 180°C/fan 160°C/gas mark 4. Grease and line two 18cm round sandwich tins.

✳ Beat the butter and sugar using a wooden spoon or electric mixer until light and fluffy. Add the eggs one at a time, beating well after each addition, and adding a tablespoon of the flour with the final egg to help prevent curdling. Fold in the remaining flour until thoroughly combined.

✳ Divide the mixture between two bowls. Stir the dissolved coffee granules into one bowl and the dissolved cocoa into the other. Spoon the batters alternately into the tins in lines. Using a knife, draw a figure of eight through the striped mixture to create a marbled effect.

✳ Bake the cakes for 20–25 minutes, until the tops spring back when lightly pressed. Leave to cool in the tins for a few minutes before turning out on to a wire rack to cool completely.

✳ Meanwhile, make the buttercream. Beat the butter until smooth, then add the remaining ingredients a little at a time until you reach a spreadable consistency.

✳ To assemble, spread a layer of buttercream over one of the cooled sponges, then top with the other sponge and cover the top and sides of the whole cake with the remaining buttercream.

Vanilla & Coconut Cake

LYNN HILL

Inspired by memories of my mother's baking, I created this cake for a CCC event with the theme 'Cakes From Our Childhoods'. My mother would bake regularly, everything from little fondant fancies to large buttercream-filled treats for our Sunday tea. This was one of my favourites. As an alternative to the coconut, coating this cake with crushed hazelnuts or walnuts also works nicely. See photo on page 24.

SERVES 10–12

170g butter, softened

170g caster sugar (vanilla caster sugar is best)

3 eggs

170g self-raising flour

50g desiccated coconut

1 tsp vanilla paste or vanilla extract, or the scraped seeds of 1 vanilla pod

1–2 tbsp milk

about 60g toasted coconut chips or desiccated coconut, to decorate

Filling & Frosting:

115g butter, softened

55g icing sugar

scraped seeds of 1 vanilla pod

225g full-fat cream cheese, chilled

2 tbsp strawberry jam (optional)

✳ Preheat the oven to 180°C/fan 160°C/gas mark 4. Grease and line two 18cm round sandwich tins.

✳ Beat the butter and sugar using a wooden spoon or electric mixer until light and fluffy. Add the eggs one at a time, beating well after each addition, and adding a tablespoon of the flour with the final egg to help prevent curdling.

✳ Fold in the remaining flour until thoroughly combined. Gently add the coconut and vanilla, then slowly add as much of the milk as you need to reach a dropping consistency.

✳ Divide the mixture between the tins, spreading it evenly. Bake for 20 minutes or until a skewer inserted into the centre comes out clean. Leave to cool in the tins for a few minutes before turning out on to a wire rack to cool completely.

✳ Meanwhile, make the frosting by beating together the butter and icing sugar until thoroughly combined. Add the vanilla seeds, then the cream cheese and mix well.

✳ Spread a thin layer of frosting over one sponge and a layer of jam, if using, over the other, then sandwich the sponges together. Cover the top and sides of the cake with the remaining frosting, then sprinkle with the coconut.

Strawberry Swiss Roll

LYNN HILL

This very easy recipe uses whisked egg whites to lighten the sponge, and vanilla seeds which bring out the summer flavours. Rolling the sponge in baking paper and leaving to cool helps make it easier to re-roll with the filling later on. The cake will keep for a day or two in the fridge, but it's best eaten on the day it's made.

SERVES 8

3 large eggs, separated
170g golden caster sugar
scraped seeds of 1 vanilla pod
100g self-raising flour
icing sugar, to dust

Filling:

250g strawberries, hulled
a little icing sugar
300ml whipping or double
   cream
scraped seeds of 1 vanilla pod

TIP

For a Lemon Swiss Roll, replace the strawberry filling with lemon curd, the vanilla seeds in the sponge with the grated zest of 2 lemons, and the vanilla seeds in the cream with the grated zest of 1 lemon.

* Preheat the oven to 200°C/fan 180°C/gas mark 6. Grease and line a 32 x 23cm Swiss roll tin.

* Beat the egg yolks and 140g of the sugar together using a hand whisk or electric mixer until light, fluffy and doubled in volume, then fold in the vanilla seeds.

* In a clean bowl, whisk the egg whites, gradually adding the remaining 30g of sugar, until soft peaks form.

* Carefully fold two-thirds of the egg white mixture into the egg yolk mixture, then fold in the flour. Fold in the remaining egg whites until thoroughly combined, then pour all the mixture evenly into the tin, smoothing the top. Bake for 10–12 minutes or until a skewer inserted into the centre comes out clean. Leave to cool in the tin for a few minutes.

* Place a fresh sheet of non-stick baking paper over the top of the sponge and turn it over, removing the baking tin and carefully peeling off the old baking paper. Beginning with the short side, gently start to roll the sponge, including the paper, so that it's rolled up with the paper. Leave to cool completely. The sponge will keep overnight if needed.

* For the filling, put about 75g of the strawberries into a food processor or blender and purée until smooth. Strain through a sieve and sweeten with icing sugar, to taste. Slice the remaining strawberries thinly and stir into the purée.

* Whip the cream until it forms soft peaks, then stir through the vanilla seeds. Carefully unwrap the sponge but leave it on the baking paper, you will need this for rolling later. Spread the whipped cream evenly over the sponge, then add the strawberry mixture.

* Here comes the fun bit. Using the baking paper as an aid, roll up the cake around the filling, taking care not to roll up the paper as well. Dust with icing sugar and serve.

Red Velvet Cake

LYNN HILL

This is a great American classic: four layers of vibrant red buttermilk sponge, filled and covered with a tangy cream cheese frosting. I recommend using concentrated gel or paste colouring, rather than the liquid variety, as this helps to create a richer colour without affecting the texture of the cake batter. The sponge is so moist that the frosted cake will keep nicely for several days if stored in an airtight tin or container.

SERVES 14–16

250g self-raising flour

1 tsp baking powder

2 tbsp cocoa powder, sifted

240ml buttermilk

1½ tsp red gel food colouring

120g butter, softened

300g golden caster sugar

2 eggs

1 tbsp vanilla extract

40g dried cranberries, finely chopped, or red sprinkles, to decorate

Cream Cheese Frosting:

275g butter, softened

145g icing sugar, sifted

2 tsp vanilla extract

450g full-fat cream cheese

TIP

Coating this cake in two layers of frosting helps prevent the coloured sponge from showing through. The first layer is called a 'crumb coat' as it catches the loose crumbs so that they don't create lumps or bumps; the second layer gives a smooth, professional-looking finish.

* Preheat the oven to 200°C/fan 180°C/gas mark 6. Grease and line two 20cm round sandwich tins.

* Mix the flour, baking powder and cocoa together, then set aside. In a separate bowl, combine the buttermilk with the red colouring and mix thoroughly.

* Beat the butter and sugar using a wooden spoon or electric mixer until light and fluffy. Add the eggs one at a time, beating well after each addition. If the mixture looks as if it's curdling, just add a tablespoon of the flour mixture. Then add the vanilla extract, half the flour mixture and half the red buttermilk and mix together. Add the remaining flour and red buttermilk mixtures and beat until well combined.

* Divide the mixture between the cake tins, spreading it evenly. Bake for 15–20 minutes, until a skewer inserted into the centre comes out clean. Leave to cool in the tins for a few minutes then turn out on to a wire rack to cool completely.

* Meanwhile, make the frosting. Beat the butter and icing sugar together until light and fluffy, then add the vanilla extract and cream cheese and beat until well combined.

* Slice the two sponges in half horizontally, creating four layers in total. Place one layer of sponge onto a plate and cover with a layer of frosting. Top with a second sponge layer and cover this with frosting, then repeat the process. Using a palette knife, cover the sides and top of the cake with a thin layer of frosting (see Tip). Leave to chill in the fridge for about an hour, until firm and set.

* Remove from the fridge then cover the whole cake with the remaining frosting. Decorate the top with a circle of cranberries or red sprinkles.

Soured Cream Coffee Cake

LISA GAIR

Another American classic, this type of 'coffee cake' isn't actually coffee-flavoured! It's so-called because it's perfect eaten warm with a nice cup of coffee. This version is filled with cinnamon and chopped pecans, but you can vary the combination of nuts and spices to your taste – just keep to the same overall quantities and remember to chop the nuts finely.

SERVES 10–12

250g butter, softened

550g granulated sugar

2 extra-large eggs

250g plain flour

300ml soured cream
  or buttermilk

1 tbsp vanilla extract

1 tbsp baking powder

pinch of salt

220g nuts (such as pecans,
  walnuts, almonds,
  hazelnuts), finely chopped

1 tbsp ground cinnamon

* Preheat the oven to 190°C/fan 170°C/gas mark 5. Grease and flour a 2.5-litre bundt tin or a 25cm savarin tin.

* Beat the butter and 400g of the sugar using a wooden spoon or electric mixer until light and fluffy. Add the eggs one at a time, beating well after each addition, and adding a tablespoon of the flour with the final egg to help prevent curdling.

* Add the soured cream and vanilla extract. Sift in the remaining flour, baking powder and salt and continue to beat gently until combined.

* In a separate bowl mix the remaining 150g of the sugar with the nuts and cinnamon.

* Pour about half the cake batter into the tin and spread evenly. Sprinkle half the nut mixture evenly over the batter, then cover with the remaining batter, spread it evenly and top with most of the remaining nut mixture, saving just a little to sprinkle over the finished cake. Press the nuts down very gently so that they stick.

* Bake for 1 hour or until a skewer inserted into the centre comes out clean. Leave to cool in the tin for 10 minutes before turning out on to a wire rack to cool completely. Sprinkle the remaining nut mixture on top and serve warm with a cup of coffee.

An all-American treat!

One of our first Clandestine events was
held in a lovely old shopping arcade in Leeds,
with Vivaciously Victorian as the theme.
The Victorians were pretty adventurous bakers,
inspired by the exciting new ingredients arriving
from across the empire, such as tropical fruits
and exotic spices. Many cake recipes that we
now think of as 'traditional' were new and
unusual back then! In this chapter you'll find
some authentic Victorian recipes, and others that
have been created by members using popular
ingredients from the day.

The Victorians also loved pies and tarts,
but as these are against CCC rules, some bakers
have turned tarts on their head, giving them a
clever twist as cake! Over 100 years later, all of
these cakes and flavours give a comforting
taste of a bygone era.

Cherry Cake

LYNN HILL

My cherry cake has long been a firm family favourite. I recommend chopping the cherries then washing and drying them thoroughly before adding to the mixture. This helps prevent them sinking to the bottom during baking. This cake keeps well for a couple of days in an airtight tin, but is nicest enjoyed while still warm. Try using dark muscovado sugar for a more intense toffee flavour. See photo on page 38 (top).

SERVES 10–12

175g butter, softened
175g light muscovado sugar
3 eggs
250g self-raising flour
200g glacé cherries, chopped,
   washed and dried

✳ Preheat the oven to 190°C/fan 170°C/gas mark 5. Grease and line a 20cm round, springform cake tin.

✳ Beat the butter and sugar using a wooden spoon or electric mixer until light and fluffy. Add the eggs one at a time, beating well after each addition, and adding a tablespoon of the flour with the final egg to help prevent curdling.

✳ Sift in the remaining flour and fold in using a large metal spoon until thoroughly combined. Add the glacé cherries. Spoon the mixture into the tin, spreading it evenly.

✳ Bake for 40–50 minutes or until a skewer inserted into the centre comes out clean. Leave to cool in the tin for a few minutes then turn out on to a wire rack and leave to cool a little further – though this cake is delicious served while still slightly warm.

Caraway Seed Cake

JOANNE JESSOP

Joanne may run her cake club on a sunny Caribbean island, but this cake was inspired by her Lancashire childhood and her auntie's baking. Caraway seeds have a distinctive savoury flavour with a hint of sweetness, and they marry nicely with orange zest. Traditionally served with a glass of Madeira or sherry, this cake is also perfect with a fresh pot of tea. It freezes very well if you want to save some for a later date. See photo on page 38 (far left).

SERVES 8–10

120g butter
120g golden caster sugar
3 large eggs
170g self-raising flour
1–2 tsp caraway seeds, according to taste
grated zest of 1 orange
50g ground almonds
2–3 tbsp milk
2 tbsp demerara sugar

TIP
Instead of the demerara topping, try drizzling over some thin glacé icing once the cake is cool (see page 248).

* Preheat the oven to 170°C/fan 150°C/gas mark 3½. Grease and line a 20cm round sandwich tin.

* Beat the butter and sugar using a wooden spoon or electric mixer until light and fluffy. Add the eggs one at a time, beating well after each addition, and adding a tablespoon of the flour with the final egg to help prevent curdling.

* Sift in the remaining flour, add the caraway seeds, orange zest and ground almonds and fold in until thoroughly combined. Add two tablespoons of milk or a little more, if necessary, to reach a dropping consistency.

* Pour the mixture into the tin, spreading it evenly, then scatter over the demerara sugar. Bake for 25–30 minutes, until a skewer inserted into the centre comes out clean.

* Leave to cool in the tin for about 5 minutes, then carefully turn out on to a wire rack to cool completely.

Cranberry & Orange Madeira Cake

DENA HABASHI-AYUB

This recipe was handed down to Dena from her mother and is a twist on the classic Madeira cake, using oil instead of butter. Beautiful, moist and easy to make, it can be adapted to your liking using other dried fruits in place of the cranberries if wished. See photo on page 39.

SERVES 10–12

360g self-raising flour
1 tsp baking powder
150g caster sugar
200ml vegetable oil
1 tsp vanilla extract
200ml freshly squeezed
   orange juice
grated zest of 2 oranges
3 eggs
50g dried cranberries

* Preheat the oven to 200°C/fan 180°C/gas mark 6. Grease and line a 23cm round, springform cake tin. Sift the flour and baking powder into a large mixing bowl and set aside.

* Place the sugar, oil, vanilla extract, orange juice and zest and eggs in a blender and blend on a medium speed for about 2–3 minutes, until well combined. Be careful not to overmix. Add the cranberries and blend for a few seconds more.

* Pour the blended mixture over the flour and fold in with a large metal spoon until thoroughly combined. Pour the mixture into the cake tin, spreading it evenly.

* Bake for 40–45 minutes, until golden brown and a skewer inserted into the centre comes out clean. Leave to cool in the tin for a few minutes before turning out on to a wire rack to cool completely.

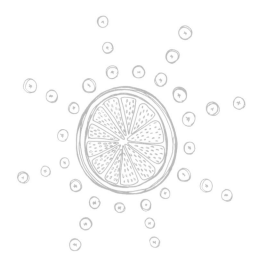

Rhubarb & Custard Cake

GARY MORTON

This scrumptious cake celebrates wonderful British rhubarb, which has been grown in the famous Yorkshire Triangle since Victorian times. It is topped with bejewelled crystallised rhubarb. The forced variety is best for decoration as it is normally a richer pink colour than field-grown rhubarb stalks.

SERVES 8–10

1 rhubarb stick, about 100g, trimmed, cut into finger-length pieces
215g caster sugar
200g butter, softened
4 eggs
200g self-raising flour

Custard Frosting:
200g full-fat cream cheese
100g butter, softened
130g icing sugar
4 tbsp ready-made custard

Decoration:
½ rhubarb stick (about 50g), trimmed, cut into finger-length pieces and thinly sliced lengthways (preferably use the pinkest pieces)
100g caster sugar

* Preheat the oven to 200°C/fan 180°C/gas mark 6. Grease and line a 900g loaf tin.

* Put the rhubarb into a roasting tin and sprinkle with 15g of the sugar. Roast for 15 minutes, until soft, then remove from the oven and leave to cool. Reduce the oven setting to 180°C/fan 160°C/gas mark 4.

* Beat the butter and remaining sugar using a wooden spoon or electric mixer until light and fluffy. Add the eggs one at a time, beating well after each addition, and adding a tablespoon of the flour with the final egg to help prevent curdling. Sift in the remaining flour and gently fold in until thoroughly combined.

* Pour a third of the batter into the tin, spreading it evenly, then cover with half the rhubarb. Repeat these layers, then add the final third of the batter, smoothing the top. Bake for 45–50 minutes or until a skewer inserted into the centre comes out clean. Leave to cool in the tin for a few minutes then transfer to a wire rack and leave to cool completely.

* Meanwhile, make the frosting. Beat half the cream cheese with the butter and sugar until well combined, then add the remaining cream cheese and the custard and mix well. Spread a layer of frosting over the cooled cake; any excess can be served alongside.

* For the decoration, place the rhubarb in a pan with the sugar and four tablespoons of water and heat gently, until the sugar dissolves and the liquid begins to boil. Once the liquid starts to turn golden and caramelise, remove the pan from the heat. Lift out the rhubarb pieces, transfer to a board and drizzle over the caramel. Drizzle any remaining caramel on to a separate board, then leave the rhubarb and caramel to set and cool.

* Once cool, arrange the caramelised rhubarb on top of the cake. The caramel can be snapped into small pieces and used for decoration too.

Battenberg Cake

SALLY HARVEY

This traditional pink and pale yellow, almond-flavoured cake was originally created in 1884 for the wedding of Queen Victoria's granddaughter to Prince Louis of Battenberg, and soon became a favourite teatime treat in drawing rooms and parlours across Britain. For a very easy decoration, crimp along the edges with a fork or your fingers.

SERVES 8–10

175g butter or margarine

175g caster sugar

3 eggs

125g self-raising flour, sifted

½ tsp vanilla extract

¼ tsp almond extract

50g ground almonds

pink food colouring

½ jar apricot jam

1 x 500g pack of white marzipan

icing sugar, to roll out the marzipan

> **TIP**
> You can buy specially designed tins for making Battenberg cake, which helps make the process a little easier.

* Preheat the oven to 180°C/fan 160°C/gas mark 4. Grease and line a 25 x 18cm rectangular cake tin. It is easiest to line it first in one direction and then the other, using two separate pieces of paper. Allow plenty of extra length on the top piece.

* Fold a pleat in the middle of the top layer of paper, to the same height as the tin, to split the tin in half. Slide a piece of cardboard into the fold to provide support while the cake is in the oven and ensure the two sides of the sponge stay straight.

* Beat the butter and sugar using a wooden spoon or electric mixer until light and fluffy. Add the eggs one at a time, beating well after each addition, and adding a tablespoon of the flour with the final egg to help prevent curdling. Add the vanilla and almond extracts, then fold in the remaining flour and ground almonds until thoroughly combined.

* Spoon half the mixture into one side of the tin. Mix the pink food colouring into the remaining mixture then spoon into the other half of the tin. (If you want, you can weigh the mixture and divide in half before colouring, so both sides are exactly the same. It's not essential, but some precision here will give a better result.) Smooth each layer with a knife, making sure they are roughly level.

* Bake for 25–30 minutes, until the sponges are springy to the touch and a skewer inserted into the centre comes out clean. Leave to cool in the tin for a few minutes, then turn out on to a wire rack, carefully peel off the baking paper and leave to cool completely.

CONTINUED

* Gently heat the jam in a small saucepan, until runny, then remove from the heat and pass through a sieve. Trim and neaten the sponges with a sharp knife, trim the top so that it is flat, then cut each sponge in half lengthways – you should have four blocks that are exactly the same length and width.

* Lay a pink piece and a yellow piece side by side then brush jam in between to stick them together, and brush more jam over the top. Stick the other two sponges together in the same way, then carefully lift this layer on top of the first to make a chequerboard pattern.

* Lightly dust a worktop with icing sugar, then roll out the marzipan until large enough to completely wrap around your cake. Trim into a long rectangle – the width of the rectangle should be the same measurement as the length of your cake. The length of the rectangle will be much longer, as the marzipan needs to reach completely round the cake so that it covers all four sides.

* Brush the marzipan with more of the warm jam, then place the assembled cake at one end so that the edges align. Roll it up slowly, neatly pressing on the marzipan. Once all four sides are covered, trim off the excess, allowing about 1cm extra for the join. Seal with a little warm water, then trim the join so that the cake sits flat. Crimp along the top edges of the cake using a crimper or your fingertips.

Date & Walnut Cake

LYNN HILL

A well-established favourite, this cake is said to have originated in Scotland during the reign of Queen Victoria. With its combination of ground almonds and a slight toffee taste from the muscovado sugar, this cake is best made a couple of days in advance to allow time for the flavours to mingle and mature. If your dates are quite dry, try soaking them in a little hot water for a few minutes until softened, then drain and pat dry before baking.

SERVES 8–10

180g butter, softened
180g light muscovado sugar
3 eggs
180g self-raising flour
½ tsp baking powder
1 tbsp milk
150g pitted dates, chopped
100g walnuts, chopped
30g ground almonds

✳ Preheat the oven to 190°C/fan 170°C/gas mark 5. Grease and line a deep 15cm round cake tin.

✳ Beat the butter and sugar using a wooden spoon or electric mixer, until light and fluffy. Add the eggs one at a time, beating well after each addition, and adding a tablespoon of the flour with the final egg to help prevent curdling.

✳ Fold in the remaining flour and baking powder until well combined. Add the milk, dates, walnuts and almonds and mix well.

✳ Spoon the mixture into the tin and bake for 1 hour or until a skewer inserted into the centre comes out clean. Leave to cool in the tin for a few minutes before turning out on to a wire rack to cool completely.

Violet Posy Cake

KAREN S. BURNS-BOOTH

This aromatic sponge cake is lightly flavoured with the old-fashioned scent of violets, which in Victorian times were associated with romance and love. Filled with a not-too-sweet mixture of citrus curd, mascarpone and violet syrup, it looks stunning decorated with sugarpaste flowers and orange zest, or crystallised violets if you prefer.

SERVES 10–12

225g butter, softened

225g caster sugar (or violet sugar if you can source it)

grated zest of 2 large oranges and juice of 1, plus extra strands of orange zest, to decorate

4 large eggs, beaten

225g self-raising flour, sifted

3 tbsp violet syrup

sugarpaste flowers (see Tip), to decorate

Filling & Frosting:

225g mascarpone cheese

3 tbsp lemon curd or orange curd, plus 3–4 tbsp extra for spreading on the cake

violet syrup, to taste

> **TIP**
> To make sugarpaste flowers, you will need violet-coloured sugar florist paste and blossom cutters. Gently knead the florist paste until pliable, then roll it out to about 1mm thick on a board dusted with a little icing sugar. Cut out shapes with the blossom cutters and leave to dry for a couple of hours. Arrange on the cake just before serving.

* Preheat the oven to 180°C/fan 160°C/gas mark 4. Grease and line two 20cm round sandwich tins.

* Beat the butter and sugar using a wooden spoon or electric mixer until light, fluffy and almost white in colour. Add the orange zest, then gradually beat in the eggs, beating well after each addition, and adding a tablespoon of the flour with the final addition to help prevent curdling.

* Very gently fold in the remaining flour using a large metal spoon. Finally, fold in the violet syrup. Divide the mixture between the cake tins, spreading it evenly.

* Bake for 20–25 minutes, until pale golden and a skewer inserted into the centre comes out clean. Remove from the oven and pour the orange juice over the sponges slowly, allowing them to absorb the juice. Leave the sponges to cool in the tins for 5 minutes before turning out on to a rack to cool completely.

* Meanwhile, beat the mascarpone briefly to loosen it, then beat in the lemon or orange curd. Add some violet syrup teaspoon by teaspoon until the desired taste has been achieved.

* When the cakes are cool, spread some lemon or orange curd on to one side of each sponge (this stops the mascarpone cream from making the cakes soggy). Place one sponge on to a plate, curd-side up and swirl some of the mascarpone cream over the top. Cover with the other sponge, curd-side down, then spread the remaining mascarpone cream over the top of the cake.

* Just before serving, decorate with the orange zest, sugarpaste flowers (see Tip), crystallised violets or other preserved or sugar flowers.

Elderflower Cordial Cake
WITH WHITE CHOCOLATE GANACHE

LYNN HILL

With its pretty white blossoms, the elderflower is the embodiment of a British summer and was extremely popular during the Victorian era due to its alleged healing properties. Most commonly used as a base for cordial, its distinctive flavour also works beautifully in cakes, giving a fragrant, fresh taste that goes well with other light, sweet flavours.

SERVES 12

4 large eggs, separated
230g caster sugar
2 tbsp elderflower cordial
130g self-raising flour

White Chocolate Ganache:
250g white chocolate, finely
   chopped, plus extra
   to decorate
250ml double cream

Elderflower Buttercream:
175g butter
175g icing sugar
2 tbsp elderflower cordial,
   or more to taste
squeeze of lemon juice

* Preheat the oven to 190°C/fan 170°C/gas mark 5. Grease and line two 20cm round sandwich tins.

* Beat the egg yolks and 190g of the sugar using an electric mixer until light, fluffy and doubled in volume (this can take about 10 minutes). Mix in the elderflower cordial.

* In a clean bowl, whisk the egg whites until soft peaks form, then add the remaining sugar until well combined. Carefully fold half the egg whites into the egg yolk mixture, then fold in half the flour until thoroughly combined. Repeat with the remaining egg whites and flour.

* Divide the mixture between the tins, spreading it evenly. Bake for about 25 minutes or until a skewer inserted into the centre comes out clean. Leave to cool in the tins for a few minutes before turning out on to a wire rack to cool completely.

* To make the ganache, place the white chocolate in a bowl. Heat the cream in a small saucepan until bubbles form around the edge, pour it over the chocolate and stir gently until all the chocolate has melted (if a few pieces refuse to melt, you could put the bowl in the microwave for a few seconds to reheat slightly, but be very careful not to overheat). Cover with cling film and leave at cool room temperature or in the fridge for 4–6 hours, until the ganache has a soft spreading consistency.

* To make the buttercream, beat the butter until light and fluffy, then gradually sift in the icing sugar and beat that in. Mix in the elderflower cordial a spoonful at a time. Taste and adjust the flavour with a squeeze of lemon juice and more elderflower cordial if desired.

* To assemble, sandwich the cakes together with the buttercream, then spread the ganache over the top and sides of the whole cake. Decorate with grated white chocolate, if you wish.

Ginger Syrup Cake
WITH GINGER & CINNAMON ICING

PIPPA SHARP

The ginger, cinnamon and golden syrup topping on this cake really gives it the wow factor! In Victorian times the use of ginger became very popular as it was thought to ease many ailments – people would eat a little crystallised ginger after a meal to aid digestion, and it naturally made its way into cakes.

SERVES 12–14

400g self-raising flour
200g granulated sugar
2 tsp ground ginger
2 tsp bicarbonate of soda
110g margarine
4 tbsp golden syrup
480ml hot water
2 eggs, beaten
dark chocolate shavings,
    to decorate

Buttercream Filling:
140g butter, softened
280g icing sugar
1–2 tbsp milk

Ginger & Cinnamon Icing:
25g butter
25g golden syrup
1 tsp ground ginger
½ tsp ground cinnamon
50g icing sugar

* Preheat the oven to 180°C/fan 160°C/gas mark 4. Grease and line two 20cm round cake tins at least 4cm deep. The mixture is very liquid so you will also need to pre-line them with a layer of foil to make them leakproof.

* Combine the flour, sugar, ginger and bicarbonate of soda in a bowl, then add the margarine and use your fingers to rub it in, until the mixture resembles breadcrumbs.

* Mix the syrup with the hot water, then gradually pour into the flour mixture, stirring with a wooden spoon until smooth. Mix in the beaten eggs. Divide the mixture between the tins, spreading it evenly. Bake for about 30 minutes or until golden brown and the sponges are springy to the touch. Leave to cool in the tins.

* Meanwhile, make the buttercream filling. Beat the butter in a bowl until soft. Add half the icing sugar and beat until smooth. Add the remaining icing sugar and one tablespoon of the milk and beat until the mixture is creamy and smooth. It should be a spreading consistency. Beat in the remaining milk if necessary.

* To make the icing, place all the ingredients in a pan and heat gently until the butter has melted. Mix well, then leave to cool slightly.

* To assemble the cake, turn the cooled sponges out of their tins, spread the buttercream over one, then top with the other sponge. Spread the icing over the top of the cake. When the icing has cooled and is set, decorate the cake with a sprinkling of chocolate shavings.

PHOTO, FROM TOP: GINGER SYRUP CAKE; MANCHESTER TART CAKE; RASPBERRY 'CAKEWELL'

Raspberry 'Cakewell'

AMANDA WOODWARD

Knowing pastry-based tarts are against CCC rules, Amanda found a way to reinvent this traditional pud by baking a gorgeous almond frangipane on top of a plain sponge base. In keeping with the original tart, delicious raspberry jam separates the two layers and a glacé icing is drizzled on top, although a dusting of icing sugar works well as a lighter alternative. See photo on previous page.

SERVES 12

125g butter, softened
175g caster sugar
2 large eggs
175g self-raising flour, sifted
4 tbsp milk
4 tbsp good-quality
    raspberry jam, to fill

Almond Frangipane:
125g ground almonds
50g butter
125g caster sugar
3 large eggs
¼ tsp almond essence
25g flaked almonds

Glacé Icing:
50g icing sugar
warm water, to mix

* Preheat the oven to 180°C/fan 160°C/gas mark 4. Grease and line two 23cm round, springform cake tins.

* Beat the butter and sugar using a wooden spoon or electric mixer until light and fluffy. Add the eggs one at a time, beating well after each addition, and adding a tablespoon of the flour with the final egg to help prevent curdling.

* Fold in the remaining flour until thoroughly combined, then stir in the milk. Spoon the mixture into one of the tins, spreading it evenly, then set aside.

* For the frangipane, beat together all the ingredients except the flaked almonds. Spoon into the other tin, spreading it evenly, then sprinkle the flaked almonds on top.

* Place both tins in the oven and bake for 25–30 minutes or until a skewer inserted into the centre comes out clean – the sponge layer will probably need 5 minutes longer than the frangipane. Leave the cakes to cool in their tins.

* Once cool, turn the plain sponge out on to a plate upside down, then cover it in an even layer of the raspberry jam. Turn out the frangipane and place it on top.

* Make the glacé icing by mixing 1–1½ tablespoons of warm water with the icing sugar to make a thin paste, then drizzle over the cake. Leave to cool and set before serving.

Manchester Tart Cake

JOANNE JESSOP

Sandwiched with raspberry jam and a rich, fragrant vanilla custard, then drizzled with icing and scattered with coconut, this is a lovely sponge-based alternative to the original Manchester tart, which many people will remember from childhood school dinners. Any leftover custard can be saved and eaten later with dessert! See photo on page 51.

SERVES 8–10

225g butter, softened
200g caster sugar
3 tbsp custard powder
200g plain flour
2 tsp baking powder
½ tsp bicarbonate of soda
4 large eggs
1 tsp vanilla essence
2–3 tbsp milk
5 tbsp good-quality
   raspberry jam, to fill

Custard:
250ml milk
1 vanilla pod, split lengthways,
   or 1 tsp vanilla extract
3 large egg yolks
75g caster sugar
25g cornflour

Topping:
100g icing sugar
1–2 tbsp milk
2 tbsp desiccated coconut

* Preheat the oven to 190°C/fan 170°C/gas mark 5. Grease and line two 20cm round sandwich tins.

* Using a hand whisk or electric mixer, beat together all the sponge ingredients except the milk until you have a smooth mixture, then add enough of the milk to reach a dropping consistency.

* Divide the mixture between the tins, spreading it evenly. Bake for 20 minutes or until a skewer inserted into the centre comes out clean. Leave to cool in the tins for at least 10 minutes, then turn out on to a wire rack to cool completely.

* Meanwhile make the custard filling. Place the milk and vanilla pod or extract in a saucepan with one tablespoon of cold water and slowly bring to the boil, then remove from the heat. Whisk the egg yolks with the sugar until pale and creamy, then whisk in the cornflour. Remove the vanilla pod from the milk, then pour over the egg mixture, whisking continuously.

* Pour the mixture back into the pan and place over a medium to high heat, continuing to whisk. Once the custard is thick enough to coat the back of a spoon, remove from the heat, pour into a bowl and either cover with cling film or a dusting of icing sugar – this stops a skin forming. When it has cooled a little, transfer to the fridge.

* To assemble the cake, spread the jam over one of the sponges. Beat the custard to loosen it then spread it on top of the jam. There is more than you will need so don't be tempted to add it all – you only need enough to make the filling 2–2.5cm thick. Top with the other sponge.

* For the topping, mix the icing sugar with a tablespoon of the milk, then keep adding milk until you reach the desired consistency. You want it to be fairly stiff. Spread the icing on the cake and immediately scatter over the coconut.

Sultana Cake

TINA BOURGAIZE

Dried fruits appear in many cake recipes by Mrs Beeton, the famous Victorian food writer. This easy-to-bake favourite is one such example. It can be easily adapted by replacing the sultanas with different dried fruits, chopped nuts, glacé cherries or – for a more child-friendly version – chocolate chips. To make it even more lunchbox-friendly, you can bake it as six mini loaves (reduce the cooking time to 20–25 minutes). If stored in an airtight container this cake will keep for a couple of days.

SERVES 12

185g butter, softened
185g caster sugar
3 eggs
185g self-raising flour
125g sultanas (or more if you like)

* Preheat the oven to 180°C/fan 160°C/gas mark 4. Grease and line an 18cm round, springform cake tin.

* Beat the butter and sugar using a wooden spoon or electric mixer until light and fluffy. Add the eggs one at a time, beating well after each addition, and adding a tablespoon of the flour with the final egg to help prevent curdling. Fold in the remaining flour until thoroughly combined, then stir in the sultanas.

* Spoon the mixture into the tin, spreading it evenly. Bake in the oven for about 1 hour or until a skewer inserted into the centre comes out clean. Leave to cool in the tin for a few minutes before turning out on to a wire rack to cool completely.

Light Stem Ginger Cake

LYNN HILL

This is a light, moist cake full of succulent pieces of stem ginger. It easily doubles up as a pudding or dessert, and is best served warm with a dollop of custard. In my experience, this cake is usually polished off before the spatula has even been washed up! See photo on page 56.

SERVES 12–16

180g butter, softened
180g soft light brown sugar
3 eggs
180g self-raising flour
1 heaped tsp ground ginger
  (be daring and add more
  if you like)
3 pieces of stem ginger in
  syrup, chopped, plus
  1 tbsp syrup
1 tbsp milk (optional)

✳ Preheat the oven to 180°C/fan 160°C/gas mark 4. Grease and line a shallow 23cm square cake tin.

✳ Beat the butter and sugar using a wooden spoon or electric mixer until light and fluffy. Add the eggs one at a time, beating well after each addition, and adding a tablespoon of the flour with the final egg to help prevent curdling.

✳ Fold in the remaining flour and ground ginger until thoroughly combined, then add the stem ginger syrup and two-thirds of the chopped stem ginger and mix until combined. The mixture should have a dropping consistency; add the milk, if necessary, to loosen it.

✳ Pour the mixture into the tin, spreading it evenly, then sprinkle over the remaining stem ginger. Bake for 25–30 minutes or until a skewer inserted into the centre comes out clean. Turn out on to a wire rack to cool, or serve warm as a dessert with crème fraîche or a great big dollop of custard.

Empire Cake
WITH CARDAMOM BUTTERCREAM

JINI MULUKUTLA

Rich, dark and moist, this cake contains all the flavours of a bygone era in abundance – rum, spices, dried fruit and nuts. Soaking the dried fruit for a minimum of four hours (or ideally overnight) helps bring it to plump perfection. With its exotic cardamom frosting and spectacular crown of hazelnuts, this is definitely cake royalty. Serve with a pot of Assam tea for an extra-special treat. See photo on page 57.

SERVES 12–16

300g dried fruit (an equal
   quantity of mixed fruit
   and sultanas)
6 tbsp dark rum
225g butter, softened
225g soft light brown sugar
4 large eggs
225g self-raising flour
½ tbsp baking powder
1 tsp mixed spice
½ tsp ground ginger
½ tsp ground cinnamon
pinch of salt
50g whole blanched
   hazelnuts or almonds,
   to decorate

Cardamom Buttercream:

1 tbsp cardamom seeds
100g butter, softened
225–250g icing sugar
2 tbsp milk

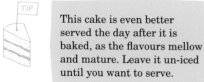

This cake is even better served the day after it is baked, as the flavours mellow and mature. Leave it un-iced until you want to serve.

* Place the dried fruit in a bowl and pour over the rum. Pour enough boiling water over just to cover the fruit. Leave to soak for a minimum of 4 hours, preferably overnight.

* Preheat the oven to 170°C/fan 150°C/gas mark 3½. Grease and line a 20cm round, springform cake tin.

* Beat the butter and sugar using a wooden spoon or electric mixer until light and fluffy. Add the eggs one at a time, beating well after each addition, and adding a tablespoon of the flour with each egg to help prevent curdling. Beat in the remaining flour, baking powder, spices and salt.

* Using a slotted spoon, remove the soaked fruit from its liquid and add to the bowl. If the batter is a bit thick, use about a tablespoon of the leftover soaking liquid to thin it out.

* Carefully fold the fruit into the cake mixture, then spoon the mixture into the tin, spreading it evenly. Bake for about 50 minutes or until a skewer inserted into the centre comes out clean or with a few crumbs clinging to it. Leave to cool in the tin for a few minutes then turn out on to a wire rack to cool completely.

* Meanwhile, make the buttercream icing. Toast the cardamom seeds in a dry frying pan for 1–2 minutes, then use a pestle and mortar to lightly crush them. Beat together the butter, icing sugar and milk until smooth, then fold in the crushed cardamom seeds.

* Once cool, cover the top and sides of the cake with the buttercream, then decorate the top with the nuts, as desired.

Earl Grey Tea Cake

MELANIE WOOD

Created for a 'Baking with Beverages' themed event, this loaf cake is a must for all tea lovers. Delicately flavoured with ground tea leaves and liberally drizzled with an Earl Grey and lemon icing, it pays homage to the British passion for tea, which is as strong now as it was in the early 1800s, when Earl Grey tea first arrived here from the Orient.

SERVES 8–10

1½ tbsp good-quality
    loose-leaf Earl Grey tea
200g plain flour
½ tsp bicarbonate of soda
120g butter
330g caster sugar
3 large eggs
120ml buttermilk
¼ tsp vanilla extract
edible flowers, to decorate

Earl Grey Icing:
100g icing sugar
grated zest of ½ lemon
about 1 tbsp strong, cold
    Earl Grey tea

＊ Preheat the oven to 180°C/fan 160°C/gas mark 4. Grease and line a 900g loaf tin then dust the insides with flour.

＊ Use a pestle and mortar to grind the tea leaves to a fine powder. Sift the ground tea, flour and bicarbonate of soda into a bowl and set aside.

＊ Beat the butter and sugar using a wooden spoon or electric mixer until light and fluffy. Add the eggs one at a time, beating well after each addition, and adding a tablespoon of the flour with the final egg to help prevent curdling.

＊ Fold in one-third of the flour mixture until thoroughly combined. Add half the buttermilk and mix well. Repeat with half the remaining flour, then add the remaining buttermilk and the vanilla extract. Mix well before adding the last of the flour and combining thoroughly.

＊ Pour the mixture into the tin and spread out evenly. Bake the cake for 40–50 minutes, until golden brown and springy to the touch. Leave to cool in the tin for 10 minutes then turn out on to a wire rack to cool completely.

＊ Once the cake is cool, make the icing. Sift the icing sugar into a bowl and add the lemon zest. Add the cold tea a little at a time, stirring thoroughly until the desired consistency is achieved.

＊ Drizzle the icing liberally and evenly over the top of the cake, letting it drip down the sides. Leave the icing to set, then decorate with edible flowers to serve.

I'm sure I'm just kidding myself but I like to think that cakes containing fruit are just a little less naughty than all the rest! So when you just have to have a treat, why not make it a fruity one?

At Clandestine events it's usually more than possible to eat the cake equivalent of your five-a-day, and in this section club members have shared some of their favourite fruity bakes. You'll find a whole orchard of ingredients, including apples and pears, peaches and plums, tangy rhubarb and sweet summer berries. They each bring different flavours, textures and colours to the cakes they're used in: so whatever your taste, and whichever fruits are in season, one of these delicious recipes is bound to tempt you.

Fruity Cakes

Plum & Cardamom Cake

LYNN HILL

If ever there were a flavour marriage made in heaven, plums and cardamom would be it. Those feeling sinful can add a splash of dessert wine to the plums while stewing them. For even more sinfulness, pour some extra wine into a glass and enjoy with a slice of this flavoursome little creature.

SERVES 8–10

200g butter, softened
200g caster sugar
3 large eggs, beaten
200g self-raising flour, sifted
¼ tsp ground cardamom

Plum Sauce:
6 plums, stoned and
    quartered
2 tbsp soft light brown sugar
¼ tsp ground cardamom
1 tbsp water or dessert wine

Cream Cheese Filling:
80g butter, softened
120g full-fat cream cheese
80g icing sugar

Glacé Icing:
about 100g icing sugar
warm water, to mix

* Preheat the oven to 190°C/fan 170°C/gas mark 5. Grease and line two 18cm round sandwich tins.

* Start by making the plum sauce. Place the plums in a pan with the sugar, cardamom and water or wine and heat gently until tender and beginning to break down. Remove from the heat, taste for sweetness and add a little more sugar if needed. Strain the liquid through a sieve set over a bowl. Set the liquid and plums to one side to cool.

* Beat the butter and sugar using a wooden spoon or electric mixer until light, fluffy and almost white in colour. Add the beaten eggs a teaspoon at a time, adding a tablespoon of the flour after each addition to help prevent curdling. Continue at intervals, until all the egg mixture and flour are combined, then mix in the cardamom.

* Divide the mixture between the tins and spread evenly. Bake for 15 minutes, until golden. Leave to cool for a few minutes in the tins, then cover one of the sponges with three-quarters of the cooled plum liquid, allowing it to soak in. Leave in the tins to cool completely.

* Make the filling by beating the butter in a bowl until smooth. Add the cream cheese and mix until combined, then sift in the icing sugar at intervals until it is all combined. Add a tablespoon of the remaining plum liquid and mix well. If the frosting is too runny, add more sifted icing sugar. Place in the fridge to firm up, especially in warm weather.

* When the sponges are completely cool, turn the plum-soaked sponge out on to a plate and cover it with the cream cheese filling, then the reserved plums. Place the other sponge on top of the filling.

* To make the glacé icing, sift the icing sugar into a bowl and gradually add about 1–1½ tablespoons of warm water to produce a runny mixture. Drizzle the icing over the cake and leave to cool and set before serving.

Overnight Tea Loaf

SHARON CLARKSON

This very simple soak-and-stir recipe is the perfect teatime treat. Try a slice with butter or even with a wedge of creamy, crumbly cheese such as Wensleydale. This cake freezes well and can be kept in an airtight tin for several days. See photo on page 89.

SERVES 10

340g mixed dried fruit (such as chopped dried apricots, sultanas, raisins, dried dates or cranberries)

55g demerara sugar

55g dark muscovado sugar

150ml tea, infused for 5 minutes, chilled

225g self-raising flour

1 large egg, beaten

＊ Put the dried fruit, sugars and tea into a bowl, stir, then leave to stand overnight. The fruit will absorb all the liquid and the flavours from the tea.

＊ Preheat the oven to 200°C/fan 180°C/gas mark 6. Grease and line a 900g loaf tin.

＊ Add the flour and egg to the steeped fruit and mix thoroughly. Pour the mixture into the loaf tin and spread out evenly. Bake the cake for 50 minutes–1 hour, until a skewer inserted into the centre comes out clean. Leave to cool in the tin for a few minutes before turning out on to a wire rack.

Fruity Lunchbox Cake

JILL EVERETT

Jill inherited this recipe from her mum, who wrote it on the back of an old Christmas card. Filled with fruit and nuts, this cake is perfect for a lunchbox or picnic, and is almost guilt-free when eaten on its own, though it's also lovely spread with butter. Do note that All-Bran works much better than bran flakes for this recipe. Deliciously moist, this cake keeps for several days if stored in an airtight tin. See photo on page 89.

SERVES 8–10

65g All-Bran

300ml semi-skimmed milk

1 banana, mashed

1 piece of stem ginger in
   syrup, thinly sliced,
   plus 2 tsp syrup

2 tbsp soft light brown sugar

1 tsp ground cinnamon

200g in total of any or
   all of the following:
   chopped dried apricots,
   chopped dates, halved glacé
   cherries, sultanas,
   chopped hazelnuts,
   chopped walnuts,
   flaked almonds

200g self-raising flour

1 heaped tsp baking powder

✳ Preheat the oven to 160°C/fan 140°C/gas mark 3. Grease and line a 900g loaf tin.

✳ Put the All-Bran, milk, banana, ginger, syrup, sugar, cinnamon and your chosen combination of fruit and nuts into a bowl, mix well and leave to stand for 1 hour.

✳ Sift the flour and baking powder into the bowl, mix well and spoon into the tin, spreading the mixture evenly. Bake for 40–45 minutes, until risen and golden. Turn out on to a wire rack, remove the baking paper and leave to cool.

Where have you 'bean' all my life?

Magic Bean Cake

SOUTH LANCASHIRE · CCC

LINDSEY BARROW

This is one of the most delicious and moist cakes you will ever taste, and the 'magic' ingredient is bound to be a talking point among your friends or guests. The haricot beans make this cake healthier than most, because you can get away with less butter yet still retain plenty of moisture. As you can imagine, the beans also give it a high fibre content! For the best flavour and the most moisture, this is best made a good 12 hours in advance of eating. You can use cannellini beans as an alternative to haricot.

SERVES 10–12

55g softened butter
  or soft margarine
225g granulated sugar
1 large egg
1 x 400g can of haricot
  or cannellini beans,
  drained, rinsed
  and mashed
1 tsp vanilla extract
225g plain flour
1 tsp ground cinnamon
pinch of ground cloves
½ tsp ground allspice
1 tsp bicarbonate of soda
½ tsp salt
3 eating apples, such as
  Cox or Golden Delicious,
  peeled, cored and diced
130g mixed dried fruit

✳ Preheat the oven to 190°C/fan 170°C/gas mark 5. Grease and line a 23cm round, springform cake tin.

✳ Beat the butter and sugar using a wooden spoon or electric mixer until light and fluffy. Beat in the egg and mix well, then add the mashed beans and vanilla.

✳ Sift the flour, spices and bicarbonate of soda into a separate bowl and mix well, then add the salt, apples and dried fruit, mixing well to coat the fruit. Add the bean mixture to the fruit mixture, mixing until thoroughly combined, then pour into the tin.

✳ Bake for 45–55 minutes, or until a skewer inserted into the centre comes out clean. Leave to cool in the tin for a few minutes then turn out on to a wire rack to cool completely.

Red Rum Raspberry Cake

PAUL BARKER

Enriched with the subtle flavours of fresh summer berries, this boozy cake combines rum and raspberries – perfect partners in crime. Rich, beautiful and decadent, with its different layers of smooth textured rum filling and white chocolate buttercream, this is perfect for any special occasion or event.

SERVES 8–10

145g butter, softened
300g caster sugar
3 eggs
370g self-raising flour, sifted
60ml milk
1 tsp red liquid food colouring
115g raspberries, plus extra
   to decorate

Rum Filling:

100g butter
125g icing sugar
3 large egg yolks
1 tbsp Bacardi rum

**White Chocolate
   Buttercream:**

125g butter, softened
125g vegetable shortening
   (Trex or Cookeen)
350g icing sugar, sifted
2 tbsp rum
60g white chocolate curls or
   grated white chocolate

TIP

Any remaining rum filling can be frozen for up to two months.

* Preheat the oven to 190°C/fan 170°C/gas mark 5. Grease and line a 20cm round, springform cake tin.

* Beat the butter and sugar using a wooden spoon or electric mixer until light and fluffy. Add the eggs one at a time, beating well after each addition, and adding a tablespoon of the flour with the final egg to help prevent curdling. Fold in the remaining flour. Add the milk and food colouring and stir in gently, then add the raspberries and gently blend.

* Pour the batter into the tin and spread evenly. Bake for 45–50 minutes, until the top is firm to the touch. Leave in the tin to cool.

* Make the rum filling. Melt the butter in a small saucepan. Add the icing sugar and bring to the boil, stirring continuously. It may look separated but when the liquid gets very hot it will come together into a smooth sauce.

* Place the egg yolks in a separate bowl and pour over the boiled butter mixture, a little at a time, stirring continuously. Stir in the rum, then return the mixture to the pan. Cook, stirring, over a low heat until it thickens. Cover with cling film and leave to cool.

* Make the white chocolate buttercream. Put the butter and vegetable shortening into a bowl and beat until softened. Gradually beat in the sifted icing sugar until light and fluffy, then beat in the rum. Add the white chocolate curls or grated white chocolate and gently mix in.

* To assemble, use a large serrated knife to cut the cake horizontally into three even layers. Spread half the buttercream over the bottom layer. Place the second layer on top and spread with a generous layer of the rum filling. Cover with the final layer and spread the remaining buttercream over the top of the cake, then decorate with fresh raspberries.

* Gently reheat the remaining rum filling and add a little water, if necessary, to give a thick pouring consistency. Drizzle some warm rum filling over the cake.

Pear & Apricot All-in-one Cake

CLARE LLEWELLYN WEST

This combination of pear and apricot creates a surprising flavour that turns this cake into something special – especially once filled with apricot jam and fruit-flavoured butter icing. It is best made with soft, ready-to-eat dried fruits and premium fresh fruit juices.

SERVES 8–10

50g dried pears,
  finely chopped
50g soft dried apricots,
  finely chopped
about 100ml apple
  juice or apricot juice
  or apple and pear juice,
  for soaking the fruit
200g plain flour
3 tsp baking powder
2 tsp ground cinnamon
200g softened butter
  or soft margarine
150g caster sugar
50g soft dark brown sugar
4 large eggs
4 tbsp apricot jam, to fill

Fruity Buttercream:
50g butter
150g icing sugar, sifted
2–3 tbsp fruit juice
  (as above)

* Preheat the oven to 170°C/fan 150°C/gas mark 3½. Grease and line two 20cm round sandwich tins.

* If the fruit is very dry soak for 20 minutes or so in fruit juice or a little hot water. Drain thoroughly, sprinkle a spoonful of the flour over the fruit and stir it to coat lightly. (This stage is not necessary if using soft, ready-to-eat fruit but pears aren't commonly sold in that form.)

* Sift the remaining flour, baking powder and cinnamon into a mixing bowl. Beat in the butter or margarine, sugars and eggs until smooth. If the consistency is stiff add a tablespoon of fruit juice and mix again. Gently stir in the fruit. Divide the mixture between the tins, spreading it evenly.

* Bake for 25–35 minutes, until well risen, firm to the touch and beginning to shrink from the sides of the tin. Turn out on to a wire rack and leave to cool completely.

* Meanwhile, make the buttercream. Beat the butter until smooth, then gradually beat in the sifted icing sugar. Add enough fruit juice to achieve a soft creamy consistency.

* To assemble, spread a layer of apricot jam over one side of each cake, then sandwich with the buttercream.

Dorset Apple Cake

KAREN S. BURNS-BOOTH

Sharp-tasting cooking apples such as Bramleys work best in this regional favourite, which is simple to make and especially popular during the harvest season. A slice of this is perfect for lunchboxes, picnics or as a comforting autumnal dessert, and it can also be baked in a tray for easy slicing into bars.

SERVES 8–10

450g cooking apples,
    such as Bramley, peeled,
    cored and thinly sliced
juice of ½ lemon
225g butter, softened
280g golden caster
    sugar
4 large eggs
340g self-raising flour
2 tsp vanilla extract
2 tbsp demerara sugar

* Preheat the oven to 190°C/fan 170°C/gas mark 5. Grease and line a 23cm round, springform cake tin.

* Place the apples in a shallow bowl, pour over the lemon juice to stop them discolouring and set aside.

* Beat the butter and sugar using a wooden spoon or electric mixer until light and fluffy. Add the eggs one at a time, beating well after each addition, and adding a tablespoon of the flour with the final egg to help prevent curdling. Beat in the vanilla extract, then sift in the remaining flour and fold in until thoroughly combined.

* Spoon half of the mixture into the tin, spreading it evenly, then arrange half the apple slices over the top of the mixture. Repeat these layers, then sprinkle over the demerara sugar.

* Bake for about 1 hour or until golden brown and a skewer inserted into the centre comes out clean. If the cake starts to get too dark before it is cooked through, cover it with foil. Leave to cool completely in the tin before turning out. If you wish to serve the cake warm as a pudding, leave to cool in the tin for 5–10 minutes, then turn out, cut into squares and serve with cream, custard or ice cream.

PHOTO, FROM LEFT: DORSET APPLE CAKE; SPICY PEAR CAKE

Spicy Pear Cake

LYNN HILL

The combination of spices and firm pears in this cake is divine and it's perfect as a comforting dessert. This is best eaten on the day it is made, either plain or with delicious cinnamon cream cheese frosting. You can vary the recipe with other firm fruits, such as apples or quinces, and you can experiment with different spices to complement them. See photo on previous page.

SERVES 6–8

2 firm sweet pears, such as Comice, peeled, cored and cut into quarters

juice of ½ lemon

115g butter, softened

115g light muscovado sugar

2 eggs, lightly beaten

1 tbsp buttermilk

115g self-raising flour, sifted

½ tsp ground cinnamon

⅛ tsp freshly grated nutmeg

Cinnamon Frosting (optional):

115g butter, softened

170g full-fat cream cheese, from the fridge

60g icing sugar, sifted

¼ tsp ground cinnamon, or more according to taste

TIP

Full-fat cream cheese straight from the fridge provides the best flavour and texture for cream cheese frosting. The butter should be beaten for a few minutes before adding the cream cheese to help prevent any lumps forming, which can be very difficult to correct. Icing sugar should always be sifted before being added, again to avoid lumps.

* Preheat the oven to 190°C/fan 170°C/gas mark 5. Grease and line a 20cm round, loose-bottomed cake tin. Place the pears in the lemon juice mixed with a little cold water to prevent them from discolouring.

* Beat the butter and sugar using a wooden spoon or electric mixer until light and fluffy. Combine the eggs with the buttermilk, then gradually add to the sugar and butter, beating well after each addition.

* Add the flour and spices at intervals to prevent curdling and continue beating until everything is thoroughly combined. Spoon the mixture into the tin and spread evenly. Drain and pat the pears dry, then place on top of the batter. The pears will sink slightly during baking.

* Bake for 20–25 minutes, until golden and a skewer inserted into the centre comes out clean. Leave the cake to cool in the tin, before turning it out on to a serving plate.

* Meanwhile, make the cinnamon frosting, if using. Beat the butter in a bowl until smooth. Add the cream cheese and mix until combined, then sift in the icing sugar and cinnamon at intervals until it is all combined. Once the cake is cool, spread the frosting over the top. Or you can leave the cake plain and serve it with thick cream or crème fraîche.

Blueberry, Peach & Amaretto Cake

JINI MULUKUTLA

This little beauty will make your taste buds tingle. Sharp, juicy blueberries, velvety sweet peaches and warming amaretto liqueur all work in perfect harmony, and a topping of amaretti biscuits adds a delicious nutty bite. Blackcurrants make a great alternative to blueberries if you want to vary the recipe.

SERVES 12–16

250g butter
125g golden caster sugar
125g light muscovado sugar
4 large eggs
175g self-raising flour
75g ground almonds
pinch of salt
50ml amaretto
2 fresh peaches, diced
200g fresh blueberries or
  defrosted frozen blueberries
5–6 amaretti biscuits,
  crushed, plus extra
  whole biscuits, to decorate

Blueberry Sauce:
1 vanilla pod, split
  lengthways
200g blueberries,
  fresh or frozen
3 tbsp caster sugar
1 strip lemon peel
125g icing sugar

* Preheat the oven to 190°C/fan 170°C/gas mark 5. Grease and line a 20cm round, springform cake tin.

* Beat the butter and sugars using a wooden spoon or electric mixer until light and fluffy. Add the eggs one at a time, beating well after each addition, and adding a tablespoon of the flour with the final egg to help prevent curdling.

* Fold in the remaining flour, ground almonds and salt until thoroughly combined. Gently mix in the amaretto, peaches and blueberries. Spoon the mixture into the tin, spreading it evenly.

* Bake for 50 minutes–1 hour, until a skewer inserted into the centre comes out clean. Leave in the tin to cool completely.

* To make the blueberry sauce, scrape the vanilla seeds from the pod and place both the seeds and pod in a small saucepan with the blueberries, sugar and lemon peel. Add 100ml water, place on a low heat, then cover and cook, crushing the blueberries occasionally. Cook until the berries have completely broken down and a runny sauce has formed.

* Remove from the heat, then lift out the vanilla pod and lemon peel and allow the sauce to cool. When cool, add the icing sugar and beat in well. If it is too thick, add a little water, a drop at a time, until it is of a drizzling consistency.

* When ready to serve, drizzle over the blueberry sauce (be as generous with it as you want), then sprinkle over the crushed amaretti. Decorate the cake with the whole amaretti.

Strawberry & Pistachio Revani

MATT FRIEND

This traditional Greek-style honey cake is made with olive oil and medium-ground polenta, which gives it a crumbly texture and helps it stay fresh for days. Pistachios add interesting colour and a lovely crunch. Close your eyes while eating and let yourself be transported to a remote Greek island in the sun!

SERVES 15

200g medium ground polenta (fine ground is okay but don't use coarsely ground)

200g vanilla sugar or caster sugar

100g self-raising flour

100g ground almonds

50g pistachios, roughly chopped

½ tsp baking powder

pinch of salt

4 large eggs

200g Greek yoghurt

200ml light olive oil (not extra virgin)

grated zest of 2 large oranges

100g ground pistachios, to decorate

Strawberry Syrup:

100g strawberries, hulled, roughly chopped

juice of ½ orange

120ml clear honey

* Preheat the oven to 180°C/fan 160°C/gas mark 4. Grease and line a 23cm round, springform cake tin, then dust the inside with flour or sprinkle with polenta.

* Combine all the dry ingredients in a large bowl. In a separate jug, mix together the eggs, yoghurt, olive oil and orange zest. Add to the dry ingredients and mix well. Pour the batter into the tin and spread out evenly.

* Bake in the oven for about 40 minutes or until a skewer inserted into the centre comes out clean. Leave the cake to cool completely in the tin.

* To make the syrup, put the strawberries into a blender and blitz to a smooth purée. Transfer to a small saucepan set over a medium heat, add the orange juice and slowly bring to the boil. Reduce the heat to low and simmer for 5 minutes, or until the syrup just begins to thicken. Add the honey and mix well, then return to the blender and blitz until smooth.

* Using a skewer or a small knife, poke holes in the top of the cooled sponge (make sure there are plenty, to soak up the honey and strawberry flavours), then pour over the hot syrup. When all the syrup has been absorbed, sprinkle over the ground pistachios. If you like, drizzle some more honey on top. Cut it into small portions to serve, ideally with a coffee.

Apricot Cake

MIKE WALLIS

Fresh apricots are a must for this gorgeous cake – try and get beautiful flushed pink ones if you can. You can cut the apricots into slices if you wish, to help prevent them sinking to the bottom during baking. It's important to pour the batter into the tin slowly to help keep as much air in the mixture as possible, which will result in a lighter sponge. Serve warm with fresh whipped cream.

SERVES 10–12

140g softened butter or
  soft margarine

125g caster sugar

2 tbsp apricot jam, plus
  extra to glaze (optional)

4 large eggs, separated

1 tsp fresh lemon juice

170g plain flour, sifted

7–8 fresh apricots, halved

icing sugar, to dust
  (optional)

double cream, whipped,
  to serve

✳ Preheat the oven to 190°C/fan 170°C/gas mark 5. Grease and line a 25cm round, loose-bottomed cake tin.

✳ Beat the butter, sugar and jam using a wooden spoon or electric mixer until light and fluffy.

✳ Add the egg yolks one at a time, beating well after each addition, until thoroughly combined.

✳ In a clean bowl, whisk the whites with the lemon juice until soft peaks form (the lemon juice stops the whites collapsing). Add a large spoonful of the whites to the egg yolk mixture and stir in roughly to loosen it, then fold in the remaining whites using a large metal spoon.

✳ Gently fold in the sifted flour in three batches, until thoroughly combined, then pour the mixture slowly into the tin, being careful not to knock it too much. Arrange the apricots over the mixture, skin-side up, covering the whole surface. Bake for 45–55 minutes or until golden brown and springy to the touch. Leave to cool in the tin for 10 minutes.

✳ Meanwhile, if you wish to glaze the cake, heat two tablespoons of apricot jam in a small saucepan with one teaspoon of water, then pass through a sieve. Turn the cake out of its tin and use a pastry brush to cover the top of the cake with the glaze. Dust with icing sugar, if you wish, and serve warm with whipped cream.

Blackcurrant & Lemon Layer Cake

LYNN HILL

This cake is best made with fresh or unsweetened blackcurrants; their tartness helps balance the sweetness of the sponge. You can also experiment with other summer fruits such as redcurrants, blueberries or raspberries. Serve dusted with icing sugar, with fresh cream on the side.

SERVES 8

250g butter, softened
250g caster sugar
4 large eggs
250g self-raising flour
grated zest of 1 lemon
50g ground almonds
100g blackcurrants
icing sugar, to dust
  (optional)

Lemon Syrup:
juice of 1 lemon
2 tsp caster sugar

Blackcurrant Jam:
500g blackcurrants
about 125g caster sugar

* Preheat the oven to 190°C/fan 170°C/gas mark 5. Grease and line three 20cm round sandwich tins.

* Beat the butter and sugar using a wooden spoon or electric mixer, until light and fluffy. Add the eggs one at a time, beating well after each addition, and adding a tablespoon of the flour with the final egg to help prevent curdling.

* Fold in the remaining flour and add the lemon zest and ground almonds, then gently mix in 100g of the blackcurrants. Divide the mixture between the tins, spreading it evenly. Bake for about 20 minutes or until pale golden, then leave to cool in the tins.

* To make the lemon syrup, gently heat the lemon juice with the caster sugar in a pan, until the sugar has dissolved and the liquid has a syrupy consistency, then remove from the heat and leave to cool. Once cool drizzle the syrup over the three sponge layers but do not oversoak them.

* To make the blackcurrant jam, place the blackcurrants and the caster sugar (add more if you prefer a sweet jam) in a pan over a low heat and cook until the fruit and sugar have formed a jam-like consistency – this will take about 5 minutes. Remove from the heat and leave to cool completely.

* To assemble the cake, turn the sponges out of their tins, spread the blackcurrant jam over two of the layers, then place one on top of the other, jam-side up. Top with the plain sponge, then finish by dusting the cake with icing sugar, if you wish.

Passion Fruit Cake

NICETTE AMMAR

This light and aromatic sponge cake is ideal as part of a spring or summer afternoon tea, especially when decorated with flowers. You can make the fruit curd in advance, or just use ready-made if you're in a hurry. You can even vary the flavour with different curds. Any leftover curd can be kept in a sterilised jar in the fridge for a couple of weeks and is also delicious spread on toast.

SERVES 8–10

225g butter, softened
225g caster sugar
2 heaped tbsp passion
   fruit curd (see below)
4 eggs
225g flour (ideally half plain,
   half wholemeal)
1 heaped tsp baking powder
2 tbsp milk
1 tbsp lemon juice

Filling & Topping:
100g white chocolate
100g butter, softened
160g icing sugar
3 tbsp passion fruit curd
   (see below)

Passion Fruit Curd:
3 passion fruit
1 large egg
40g caster sugar
25g butter

✳ You will need to make the passion fruit curd in advance. Cut the passion fruit in half and scoop out the flesh with a spoon. Strain the juice and flesh through a sieve to extract the seeds (you can discard them). Place the passion fruit juice, eggs and sugar in a heatproof bowl and whisk until thoroughly combined.

✳ Place the bowl over a pan of gently simmering water and whisk often and regularly – the mixture will heat and thicken, but do not overheat or you will end up with scrambled eggs. Add the butter and continue to whisk at intervals for about 20 minutes or until the mixture is thick enough to coat the back of a spoon. Pour into a sterilised jar, leave to cool, then store in the fridge until needed (no longer than two weeks).

✳ For the cake, preheat the oven to 190°C/fan 170°C/gas mark 5. Grease and line two 20cm round sandwich tins.

✳ Beat the butter and sugar using a wooden spoon or electric mixer until light and fluffy, then beat in the curd. Add the eggs one at a time, beating well after each addition, and adding a tablespoon of the flour with the final egg to help prevent curdling. Sift in the remaining flour and baking powder and fold in gently until thoroughly combined. Combine the milk and lemon juice and stir into the mixture.

✳ Divide the mixture between the tins, spreading it evenly. Bake for about 25 minutes or until a skewer inserted into the centre comes out with only a few crumbs sticking to it. Leave to cool in the tins for a few minutes then turn out on to a wire rack to cool completely.

CONTINUED ▶

✳ Meanwhile, make the filling and topping. Melt the white chocolate gently in a heatproof bowl set over a saucepan of barely simmering water. Beat the butter and sugar together in a separate bowl until light and fluffy, then mix in the melted chocolate until well combined. Finally, beat in the curd. You will need to fill and top the cake straight away as the mixture firms up as it sets.

✳ To assemble the cake, spread half the filling mixture over the top of one of the cooled sponges, then cover with the other sponge and spread the remaining mixture over the top of the cake.

BEHIND THE SCENES
at the
CLANDESTINE CAKE CLUB

the "It was Fatless Before being covered in Mascarpone & Orange & Almond Cake

Banana & Cardamom Loaf

MIKE WALLIS

The secret to success for this moist and aromatic banana loaf is the inclusion of natural yoghurt and lemon juice – they react with the bicarbonate of soda to create a really light, airy cake. It's also a great way to use up overripe bananas. Wait until it's completely cool before slicing or the cake will fall to bits.

SERVES 10

120g butter, softened

225g caster sugar

2 large eggs

300g plain flour

4 ripe bananas, mashed
(about 200g)

8 cardamom pods, seeds
removed and finely crushed
(or 1½ tsp ground
cardamom)

½ tsp salt

75ml natural yoghurt

2 tsp lemon juice

1 tsp bicarbonate of soda

Preheat the oven to 190°C/fan 170°C/gas mark 5. Grease and line a 900g loaf tin.

Beat the butter and sugar using a wooden spoon or electric mixer, until light and fluffy. Add the eggs one at a time, beating well after each addition, and adding a tablespoon of the flour with the final egg to help prevent curdling.

Add the bananas, cardamom and salt, mixing thoroughly. Beat in the yoghurt and lemon juice, then sift in the remaining flour and bicarbonate of soda and fold them in until thoroughly combined. Pour the mixture into the tin, spreading it evenly.

Bake for 1 hour, until well risen and browned on top and a skewer inserted into the centre comes out clean. Leave to cool in the tin for 2 minutes, then turn out on to a wire rack and allow to cool completely before slicing.

PHOTO: BANANA & CARDAMOM LOAF; OVERNIGHT TEA LOAF; FRUITY LUNCHBOX CAKE

Cardamom, Rose & Rhubarb Cake

VANESSA KIMBELL

Soft, sweet and perfumed, and with a tangy rhubarb jam, this whimsical cake from Vanessa's book Prepped *makes a gorgeous centrepiece for a summer tea party. Impress your guests by decorating it with flowers such as roses or geraniums. Serve it in the garden, but keep an eye on the bees, who are bound to want a slice of the action!*

SERVES 8–10

250g softened butter
or soft margarine
250g cardamom sugar
(see Tip) or 250g caster
sugar mixed with 1 tsp
freshly ground cardamom
4 large eggs
250g self-raising flour
edible rose or geranium
petals, to decorate

Rose Filling:

300ml double cream
3 drops of rose essence
50g icing sugar, sifted
200g rhubarb jam

Glacé Icing:

150g icing sugar
warm water, to mix

* Preheat the oven to 190°C/fan 170°C/gas mark 5. Grease and line two 20cm round sandwich tins.

* Beat the butter and sugar using a wooden spoon or electric mixer until light and fluffy. Add the eggs one at a time, beating well after each addition, and adding a tablespoon of the flour with the final egg to help prevent curdling. Sift in the remaining flour and fold in with a large metal spoon until thoroughly combined.

* Divide the mixture between the cake tins, spreading it evenly. Bake in the oven for 20–25 minutes, until firm to the touch. Turn the sponges out on to a wire rack to cool completely.

* When the cakes are cool, make the filling. Whip the cream with the rose essence and icing sugar until thick. Spread the jam over the base of one sponge, then cover with the whipped cream and place the other sponge on top.

* Make the glacé icing by sifting the icing sugar into a bowl and then gradually add about 1–1½ tablespoons of warm water until you have a runny mixture. Pour the icing over the cake and leave to set before decorating with flowers or petals.

> **TIP**
>
> To make cardamom sugar, place caster sugar and cardamom pods in a jar – roughly 20 pods per 100g of sugar – and allow to infuse for about 6 weeks.

With more than ten overseas Clandestine Cake Clubs in such diverse locations as Canada, Australia, Finland and the Caribbean, we get a lot of great ideas for worldwide flavours. Many members in the UK are also inspired by global ingredients, traditions and customs. The recipes in this chapter will give you a taste of our favourite international baking, taking you around the world in an array of delicious cakes. Some flavours and spices will be quite familiar, others are more unusual and unexpected, but all are incredibly tasty.

Global
Cakes

Dutch Speculaas

MARZIPAN-FILLED SPICED CAKE

CARLA GARDINER

This cake is traditionally baked and eaten in Holland on the feast of St Nicolas, on 5 December. Many Dutch families have their own recipe for the 'speculaaskruiden', the special spice mix that flavours the cake. This is Carla's version, which she has perfected to her taste. The cake itself keeps well for 4–5 days in a sealed tin.

SERVES 10–12

250g self-raising flour
2 tbsp speculaaskruiden (see below)
150g soft dark brown sugar
pinch of salt
150g butter, cut into small cubes
2 tbsp milk
50g whole almonds, blanched, to decorate

Speculaaskruiden (spice mixture):
4 tsp ground cinnamon
½ tsp ground mace
¼ tsp each of ground cloves, ginger and nutmeg
pinch each of ground white pepper, cardamom and star anise

Marzipan Filling:
115g icing sugar
250g ground almonds
1 large egg, beaten
2 tsp lemon juice

* Preheat the oven to 170°C/fan 150°C/gas mark 3½. Grease and line a 20cm round, springform cake tin, about 4cm deep.

* To make the speculaaskruiden, simply stir all the spices together until thoroughly mixed.

* For the marzipan, sift the sugar into a mixing bowl and stir in the almonds. Beat the egg well, then add half of it to the dry ingredients along with the lemon juice. Use a wooden spoon or your hands to mix to a firm paste. Depending on how much filling you like, you might find this quantity is slightly too much for this cake but marzipan will keep well in the fridge for up to a week or for several months in the freezer.

* To make the cake, combine the flour, speculaaskruiden, sugar and salt in a mixing bowl. Add the butter and use your fingertips to rub in until the mixture resembles breadcrumbs. Then add the milk and knead to a soft dough.

* Put just over half the dough into the bottom of the tin, and press it out with your fingers or the back of a spoon so it covers the base of the tin evenly and goes about two-thirds of the way up the sides.

* Dust a work surface with icing sugar and roll out the marzipan into an 18cm circle about 1cm thick. Place it in the tin. Gently roll out the remaining dough and place it on top, making sure it meets the dough at the side of the tin.

* Decorate with the almonds, then brush the cake all over with the remaining beaten egg. Bake for 30 minutes. Leave to cool in the tin for 5–10 minutes, then turn out on to a wire rack to cool completely.

Polish Apple Cake
WITH CHOCOLATE & CANDIED ORANGE

FILIP CUPRYCH

Sweet, sharp, tangy apples are the best choice for this lovely cake. This is a family recipe that was handed down to Filip from his nan, but he has since given it a few of his own additions, including a creamy filling and topping, and a scattering of candied orange peel and grated chocolate. See photo on previous page.

SERVES 8

2 eggs
125g caster sugar
175g plain flour
½ tsp bicarbonate of soda
½ tsp baking powder
100ml sunflower oil
500g eating apples, such as Cox, peeled, cored, cut into 2cm chunks

Filling & Topping:
600ml double cream
3 tbsp icing sugar
50g candied orange peel, chopped
25g milk chocolate, grated

* Preheat the oven to 180°C/fan 160°C/gas mark 4. Grease and line an 18cm square cake tin.

* Whisk the eggs with the sugar in a large bowl until pale and frothy. Sift the flour, bicarbonate of soda and baking powder into a bowl. Add them to the egg mixture in three or four batches, alternating with the oil. Add the apples and stir well to combine.

* Pour the mixture into the tin, spreading it evenly. Bake for about 45 minutes, until a skewer inserted into the centre comes out clean. Leave to cool completely in the tin.

* Once cool, turn the cake out of the tin and use a serrated knife to cut it in half horizontally. Remove the paper from the bottom half and place on a serving dish or plate.

* To make the filling and topping, whip the cream and icing sugar until the cream thickens. Spread half the cream over the bottom layer of cake then cover with the top layer. Spread the remaining cream evenly over the top and sides of the cake, then sprinkle the candied peel and grated chocolate over the top of the cake. Place in the fridge for 2–3 hours to set.

Cayman Mango Cake

JOANNE JESSOP

June is mango season in the Cayman Islands, when farmers' markets overflow with fragrant, juicy fruit. It inspired Joanne to create this rich cake, which is so moist it requires no filling or glaze. If your mango isn't juicy enough, supplement with the juice from half an orange. See photo on page 95.

SERVES 12

250g plain flour (or a mixture of plain and wholemeal)

½ tsp salt

2 tsp bicarbonate of soda

1–2 tsp ground cinnamon, according to taste

230g soft light brown sugar (or a mixture of light and dark)

230ml vegetable, rapeseed or sunflower oil

1 tsp vanilla extract

1 large, ripe mango (about 250g), peeled, stoned and diced

3 large eggs, lightly beaten

50g raisins, golden or brown

25g pecan nuts or walnuts, chopped (optional)

✳ Preheat the oven to 180°C/fan 160°C/gas mark 4. Grease and line a 20cm round, loose-bottomed cake tin.

✳ Sift the flour, salt, bicarbonate of soda and cinnamon into a large bowl. Add the sugar, then gently stir in the oil and vanilla, then the mango and eggs. Finally, fold in the raisins and nuts, if using, mixing just until everything is incorporated. Spoon the mixture into the tin, spreading it evenly.

✳ Bake for 55 minutes–1 hour, until a skewer inserted into the centre comes out clean. It is best to bake for a bit longer if you are not sure as this is a very moist cake and you don't want it to be undercooked in the middle. Leave to cool in the tin for a few minutes before turning out on to a wire rack to cool completely.

Sweet Potato & Pecan Cake

GILLIAN TARRY

A staple of traditional American cooking, the sweet potato has found its way into many delicious dishes including this delicately spiced cake. It's perfectly paired with another US favourite: pecan nuts. Walnuts or hazelnuts can be substituted for the pecans if you like, and you can also try using different spices, though be careful not to overdo it.

SERVES 8–10

150g soft light brown sugar

130ml rapeseed oil

150g puréed sweet potato (about 1 medium sweet potato, peeled, diced and steamed until tender, then puréed)

1 large egg

2 tsp vanilla extract

160g plain flour

½ tsp ground cinnamon

¼ tsp ground allspice

1 tsp baking powder

¼ tsp bicarbonate of soda

¼ tsp salt

75ml low-fat natural yoghurt

75g desiccated coconut

50g pecan nuts, chopped, plus a few extra whole nuts, to decorate

Topping:

140g icing sugar

½ tsp vanilla extract

40g desiccated coconut, lightly toasted

* Preheat the oven to 190°C/fan 170°C/gas mark 5. Grease and line a 20cm round, springform cake tin.

* Beat the sugar, oil and sweet potato purée in a large bowl until blended and smooth. Add the egg and vanilla and beat until incorporated.

* Sift the flour, cinnamon, allspice, baking powder, bicarbonate of soda and salt into a separate bowl, then gently fold the dry ingredients into the wet together with the yoghurt. Finally, fold in the coconut and nuts.

* Pour the batter into the tin and spread it out evenly. Bake for about 35 minutes or until the top springs back when gently pressed and the edge of the cake is starting to come away from the sides of the tin. Leave to cool in the tin for 10 minutes before turning out on to a wire rack to cool completely.

* For the topping, sift the icing sugar into a bowl then add the vanilla extract and about a tablespoon of water and mix to a pouring (but not too runny) consistency, adding more water, if necessary.

* Once the cake is cool, spread the icing over the top, allowing some to drip down the sides. While still wet, sprinkle over the toasted coconut, then decorate with the whole pecans. Leave the icing to set for 1 hour before serving.

Japanese Green Tea & Orange Cake

EMMA ELLIOT

This cake was inspired by Emma's favourite cup of tea. Matcha (Japanese green tea powder) adds a delicate flavour and brings the colour of the sponge to life. The green tea flavour is beautifully complemented by orangey icing. Make sure not to overwork the mixture – any lumps will sort themselves out during baking. This cake will last for up to a week if covered and kept in an airtight container.

SERVES 12–14

250g butter, softened
250g caster sugar
4 large eggs
250g self-raising flour, sifted
4 tbsp matcha tea
1–2 tbsp milk
 (optional)

Orange Buttercream:
170g butter, softened
500g icing sugar
2–3 tbsp orange juice
grated zest of 1 orange

* Preheat the oven to 180°C/fan 160°C/gas mark 4. Grease and line two 20cm round sandwich tins.

* Beat the butter and sugar using a wooden spoon or electric mixer until light and fluffy. Add the eggs one at a time, beating well after each addition, and adding a tablespoon of the flour with the final egg to help prevent curdling. Gently fold in the matcha and remaining flour until just combined. Add a little of the milk until you reach a dropping consistency.

* Divide the mixture between the tins, spreading it evenly. Bake for 20–25 minutes, until a skewer inserted into the centre comes out clean. Leave to cool in the tins for 10 minutes before turning out on to a wire rack to cool completely.

* Meanwhile, make the buttercream. Beat the butter using an electric whisk until pale and smooth. Gradually add the icing sugar and beat until light and fluffy (you may notice it getting stiff – don't worry the mixture lightens up when you add the orange juice). Beat in the orange juice a tablespoon at a time until combined, then mix in the orange zest.

* To assemble, sandwich the cakes together with a layer of buttercream that is no more than about 1cm thick. Spread half the remaining buttercream over the top and sides of the whole cake, then transfer to the fridge to set for about 2 hours (this is the 'crumb coat', see Tip on page 30).

* Once set, use the remaining buttercream to cover the cake in a second layer. Return to the fridge for another 2 hours to set before serving.

Baked Ricotta Cheesecake

SUE ARON

Containing ricotta, mascarpone and Marsala, could this cheesecake be any more Italian? Be prepared: it does tend to drop in the middle once cooled, but this won't detract from its deliciousness, especially when you have plump Marsala-soaked cranberries, citrus zest and candied peel hidden away in the middle to keep your taste buds busy. Decorate with fresh seasonal berries piled into the central hollow.

SERVES 8–10

3 tbsp dried cranberries

3 tbsp Marsala or any good cooking sherry

250g mascarpone cheese

500g ricotta cheese

150g icing sugar, plus extra to dust (optional)

4 large eggs, beaten

finely grated zest of 1 orange

finely grated zest of 1 lemon

4 tbsp candied lemon or orange peel, chopped (optional)

50g raspberries, to decorate

50g blueberries, to decorate

* Preheat the oven to 180°C/fan 160°C/gas mark 4. Grease and line the base and sides of a 23cm round, springform cake tin.

* Put the cranberries into a bowl with the Marsala and leave to soak for 15 minutes.

* Place the mascarpone and ricotta in a large bowl and sift in the icing sugar, beating well to combine. Gradually add the eggs, beating well between each addition.

* Strain the cranberries and add to the mixture along with the orange and lemon zests and candied peel, if using. Mix to distribute evenly.

* Pour the mixture into the tin, spreading it evenly. Bake for about 40 minutes–1 hour or until the cheesecake feels just firm on top when gently pressed in the middle. Leave in the tin to cool completely, then chill before serving.

* To serve, carefully unmould the cheesecake on to a flat dish or plate and decorate the top with the raspberries and blueberries or other berries or fruit according to the season. Gently dust a little icing sugar over the top to finish, if you like.

A 'berry' good cheesecake

Amaretto Cream Cake

CARMELA HAYES

An Italian spin on the Victoria sponge, this is simplicity at its best. With crushed amaretti biscuits in the sponge and a whipped cream filling that's laced with almond liqueur, this cake is perfect with coffee, or maybe even something a teensy bit stronger!

SERVES 8–10

175g butter, softened

175g golden caster sugar

4 eggs

175g self-raising flour

55g hard amaretti biscuits, crushed

cocoa powder, to dust

Amaretto Filling:

150ml double cream

1 tbsp amaretto liqueur, or more according to taste

* Preheat the oven to 190°C/fan 170°C/gas mark 5. Grease and line two 20cm round sandwich tins.

* Beat the butter and sugar using a wooden spoon or electric mixer until light and fluffy. Add the eggs one at a time, beating well after each addition, and adding a tablespoon of the flour with each egg to help prevent curdling.

* Fold in the remaining flour and crushed amaretti biscuits until thoroughly combined.

* Divide the mixture between the tins, spreading it evenly. Bake for about 20 minutes until golden. Leave in the tins to cool completely.

* For the filling, whip the cream until soft peaks form. Add the amaretto liqueur and mix well, then spread the filling over one of the cakes and top with the other. Sandwich the two cakes together, then dust the top with cocoa powder to decorate.

Lingonberry White Chocolate Cake

FINNISH CHRISTMAS CAKE

RIIKKA HARIKKALA

Sharp, red lingonberries are a real Finnish favourite – if you can get hold of them they will give this cake an authentic touch, but dried cranberries are an excellent substitute. Another Finnish staple is the pomerans – ground dried bitter orange peel. Again, it makes a lovely addition, but grated orange zest is a perfectly good alternative.

SERVES 12

3 eggs
200g caster or
   granulated sugar
90ml rapeseed oil
1 tsp vanilla extract
120g crème fraîche
225g plain flour
1½ tsp pomerans (ground
   dried bitter orange peel)
   or grated zest of 1 orange
½ tsp baking powder
¼ tsp bicarbonate of soda
pinch of salt
1½ tsp ground cinnamon
140g dried lingonberries or
   dried cranberries, chopped
juice of 1 orange

Amaretto Icing:

120g butter, at room
   temperature
50ml milk
500g icing sugar, sifted
1 tbsp amaretto liqueur

Filling:

125g white chocolate
60ml double cream

⁕ Preheat the oven to 175°C/fan 155°C/gas mark 4. Grease and line two 20cm round sandwich tins.

⁕ Whisk the eggs and sugar in a large bowl until light and fluffy. Add the oil a drop at a time, whisking continuously. Combine the vanilla with the crème fraîche, then add to the egg mixture in small amounts – roughly a tablespoon at a time, mixing well after each addition.

⁕ In a separate bowl, combine the flour, pomerans or orange zest, baking powder, bicarbonate of soda, salt and cinnamon. Gently fold the dry mixture into the egg mixture until thoroughly combined. Scatter the lingonberries over the batter and mix gently.

⁕ Spoon the batter into the tins and spread evenly. Bake for 20 minutes, until golden on top and a skewer inserted into the centre comes out clean. Leave to cool in the tins for a few minutes, then turn out on to a wire rack. When completely cool, douse the cakes with the orange juice.

⁕ For the icing, beat the butter, milk and half the icing sugar until soft and creamy. Add the rest of the icing sugar, and beat again until well combined. Set aside 100g of the plain icing to use in the filling, then add the amaretto to the remainder and beat well.

⁕ To make the filling, melt the chocolate in a bowl set over a pan of gently simmering water, making sure the water does not touch the base of the bowl. Remove from the heat and set aside to cool to room temperature.

⁕ When the chocolate has cooled, place it with the cream and the reserved plain icing in a large bowl and beat until the mixture becomes light and creamy. Put in the fridge for 30 minutes or so to firm up, before using to sandwich the cakes together.

⁕ Finally, use the amaretto icing to cover the cake all over. Decorate with a few dried lingonberries or cranberries on top, if you wish.

Caribbean Spiced Rum Cake

KAREN JEFFERSON

If you love rum, you'll love this super-moist cake. Karen recommends using rum with a distinctive vanilla flavour, such as Sailor Jerry. Allow the cake to soak up all of the rum glaze until it cannot hold any more – this cake is not for teetotallers!

SERVES 16

300g golden caster sugar
120ml vegetable oil
3 large eggs
120ml milk
60ml dark spiced rum
  (such as Sailor Jerry)
250g plain flour
1 tsp bicarbonate of soda
pinch of salt
1 tsp ground allspice
1 tsp ground cinnamon
1 tsp freshly grated nutmeg
95g pecan nuts, chopped

Rum Glaze:
115g butter
200g golden caster sugar
170ml dark spiced rum

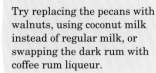

Try replacing the pecans with walnuts, using coconut milk instead of regular milk, or swapping the dark rum with coffee rum liqueur.

* Preheat the oven to 160°C/fan 140°C/gas mark 3. Grease and flour a 1.5–2-litre bundt tin.

* In a bowl or jug, whisk together the sugar, oil, eggs, milk and rum until combined.

* Mix together the flour, bicarbonate of soda, salt and spices. Make a well in the centre of the dry ingredients and pour in the rum mixture, stirring until combined. Stir in the pecans.

* Pour the batter into the tin, spreading it evenly. Bake in the oven for about 50 minutes, or until a skewer inserted into the centre comes out clean. To prepare the cake for the rum glaze, pierce the cake all over with a skewer, then leave in the tin to cool completely.

* To make the glaze, put the butter into a small saucepan along with 60ml water and bring to a slow boil. Stir in the sugar and simmer for 5 minutes, stirring occasionally. Remove from the heat and leave the mixture to cool for 5 minutes, then skim the froth from the top and stir in the rum. Leave to cool for a further 15 minutes.

* Gradually drizzle small amounts of the glaze over the top of the cake while it is still in the tin. When the cake cannot absorb any more glaze turn it out of the tin and place it upside down on to a plate. Repeat the procedure on the bottom of the cake. Let the cake sit until the glaze has soaked in. To use all of the glaze repeat the procedure from the beginning, putting the cake back into the tin to glaze the top.

* Serve with softly whipped double cream flavoured with vanilla.

Dutch Hazelnut Cake

CHRIS HOLMES

This is a seriously rich, no-holds-barred, nutty cake with an indulgent Nutella centre. It's sinful enough to be served as a dessert at a dinner party or, if you're feeling extravagant, treat yourself to a slice for breakfast.

SERVES 12–14

465g whole hazelnuts
480g unsalted butter, softened
180g caster sugar
180g soft light brown sugar
1 tsp vanilla extract
grated zest of 1 lemon
4 eggs
200g plain flour
2½ tsp baking powder

Filling & Topping:
300–400g Nutella
100g good-quality dark chocolate (min. 70% cocoa solids)
100g roasted hazelnuts, chopped

* Preheat the oven to 180°C/fan 160°C/gas mark 4. Grease and flour a 2.5–3-litre bundt tin, shaking out the excess flour.

* Using a food processor, grind the whole hazelnuts fairly finely (as fine as couscous). Set aside until needed.

* Beat the butter, sugars, vanilla and lemon zest using a wooden spoon or electric mixer until light and fluffy. Add the eggs one at a time, beating well after each addition, and adding a tablespoon of the flour with the final egg to help prevent curdling.

* In a separate bowl, sift together the remaining flour, baking powder and ground hazelnuts, then fold the dry mixture into the wet until thoroughly combined. Spoon into the tin and spread evenly.

* Bake for about 1 hour or until the cake feels springy to the touch and a skewer inserted into the centre comes out clean. Leave to cool in the tin for 15 minutes, then turn out on to a cake board or serving plate.

* When completely cool, use an apple corer to make 8–12 vertical holes in the crown of the cake at evenly spaced intervals. Go as deep into the cake as possible without touching the base board. Save the pieces of cake that are removed.

* Scoop the Nutella into a piping bag and use it to fill the holes in the cake. Cut the tops off the reserved cake trimmings and replace them on top of the Nutella.

* Melt the chocolate in a bowl set over a pan of gently simmering water, making sure the water does not touch the base of the bowl. Stir gently, then remove from the heat and spoon it all over the crown of the cake so it runs down the sides. Immediately sprinkle over the chopped hazelnuts so they stick to the chocolate. Allow the chocolate to set before serving.

Tarta de Almendras
SPANISH ALMOND CAKE

SUE ARON

An authentic Mallorcan gateau, traditionally served at fiestas, this lovely moist cake keeps well for several days. Made without butter or flour, it's suitable for dairy-free and gluten-free diets. If you can grind fresh almonds yourself, it is well worth the effort, but shop-bought ground almonds work just as well.

SERVES 10–12

300g ground almonds
finely grated zest of 1 lemon
1 tsp ground cinnamon
7 eggs, separated
300g caster sugar
icing sugar, to dust

* Preheat the oven to 190°C/fan 170°C/gas mark 5. Grease and line a 23cm round, springform cake tin.

* Mix the almonds, lemon zest and cinnamon together in a bowl and set aside. Beat the egg yolks and sugar using an electric mixer, until pale and creamy.

* In a separate bowl, beat the egg whites until soft peaks form. Fold a spoonful of the egg whites into the egg yolk mixture to loosen it, then fold in a large spoonful of the ground almonds. Add the remaining egg whites and almonds in alternate amounts and fold in, being careful not to knock the air out of the mixture.

* Carefully pour the mixture into the tin and spread evenly. Bake the cake for about 40 minutes or until a skewer inserted into the centre comes out clean. If it's not clean, return the cake to the oven for another 5–10 minutes.

* Leave to cool in the tin before turning out, then dust with icing sugar. Serve as is or with good-quality vanilla ice cream or crème fraîche.

From Vienna,
with love x

Sachertorte
WITH CHOCOLATE ORANGE ICING

FIONNUALA LAWES

The original recipe for Sachertorte is kept hidden in a vault in Vienna's Hotel Sacher, so few people know the true combination of ingredients. Here Fionnuala has created a large, crowd-pleasing imitation with an indulgent chocolate orange icing. It is a real style piece, complete with edible gold lustre embellishment. For a personal touch, why not inscribe your own initials on the top?

SERVES 20

340g good-quality dark chocolate (min. 80% cocoa solids)

225g soft margarine or butter, softened

225g golden caster sugar

10 eggs, separated

225g self-raising flour, sifted

½ tsp vanilla extract

3 tbsp smooth marmalade (non bitter and with very fine or no bits)

edible gold lustre, to decorate (optional)

Chocolate Icing:

210ml double cream

255g dark orange chocolate (min. 55% cocoa solids), chopped

3 tsp glycerine

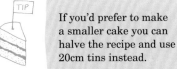

TIP
If you'd prefer to make a smaller cake you can halve the recipe and use 20cm tins instead.

* Preheat the oven to 150°C/fan 130°C/gas mark 2. Grease and line two 30cm round, loose-bottomed cake tins.

* Slowly melt the chocolate in a bowl set over a pan of gently simmering water, making sure the water does not touch the base of the bowl. Stir gently, then remove from the heat.

* Beat the margarine and sugar using an electric mixer until light and fluffy. Add the egg yolks one at a time, beating well after each addition, and adding a tablespoon of the flour with the final egg to help prevent curdling.

* Add the vanilla extract to the melted chocolate and then gradually mix this into the egg yolk mixture on a low speed. Sift in the remaining flour and fold in using a large metal spoon.

* In a scrupulously clean bowl, whisk the egg whites until stiff peaks form, then fold into the cake mixture using a large metal spoon. Divide the mixture between the tins, spreading it evenly. Bake for 40–45 minutes, until firm to the touch. Turn the cakes out upside down on to a wire rack.

* Heat the marmalade gently and stir to get a smooth consistency, then use a pastry brush to brush it over the top of one cake layer and place on a large flat plate. Place the other cake on top, upside down, so you have a flat surface for icing. Brush the remaining marmalade all round the side of the cakes. Place the cake on a wire rack set over a wipe-clean surface.

CONTINUED

✳ To make the icing, pour the cream into a pan, add the chocolate and heat gently until melted. Remove from the heat and stir until smooth, then add the glycerine. It's important that the consistency of the icing remains very runny in order to achieve a smooth, flat surface so try to do these next few steps as quickly as possible.

✳ Use a palette knife to thinly cover the sides of the cake with the icing. Pour the remaining icing directly onto the surface of the cake and use the palette knife to roughly spread the mixture over the surface of the cake, letting gravity do the work to create a perfectly flat and smooth surface. The icing should drip through the cooling rack onto the wipe-clean surface and this run-off can be used to fill any gaps.

✳ Transfer the cake to a large flat plate that will ensure the sponge is not exposed to the air and leave to set for at least 3 hours. If you have an airtight container that is large enough, that would be preferable.

✳ Decorate by applying edible gold lustre using a paint brush, if you wish, and serve with whipped cream and a pinch of fine orange zest.

English Breakfast
Earl Grey
Peppermint
Chamomile

the
SECRET
IS
OUT...

COME
BAKE
WITH
~ US ~

Torta Colombina

EUAN GREIG

This recipe was inspired by an Italian Easter treat called Colomba Pasquale ('Easter dove'), which is similar in texture to panettone. It's a rich, intensely orange-flavoured cake, which is slightly squidgy underneath and has a crunchy almond and nibbed sugar topping. For a lighter filling, simply sandwich the layers with a thin layer of orange curd.

SERVES 8–12

175g butter, softened

grated zest of 2 oranges

175g caster sugar

few drops of bitter almond extract

1 tsp real vanilla extract

3 eggs, plus 2 yolks (save the whites for the topping)

175g self-raising flour

50g ground almonds

Topping:

80g ground almonds

80g icing sugar (vanilla if possible), sifted

2 egg whites

30–40g whole almonds

30–40g pearl/nibbed sugar (or crushed sugar cubes)

Filling:

75g good-quality orange curd

60g icing sugar, sifted

 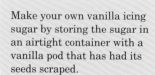

Make your own vanilla icing sugar by storing the sugar in an airtight container with a vanilla pod that has had its seeds scraped.

* Preheat the oven to 190°C/fan 170°C/gas mark 5. Grease and line two 18cm round, loose-bottomed cake tins, about 4cm deep.

* Beat the butter, orange zest and caster sugar using a wooden spoon or electric mixer until light and fluffy. Mix in the almond and vanilla extracts, then add the eggs and yolks one at a time, beating well after each addition, and adding a tablespoon of the flour with the final egg to help prevent curdling.

* Using a large metal spoon, fold in the ground almonds, then the remaining flour, until thoroughly combined. The mixture should be light but stiff. Divide the mixture between the tins, spreading it evenly.

* Make the topping by mixing the ground almonds, sifted icing sugar and egg whites until you have a rough paste. Use a teaspoon to dot this over the surface of one of the cakes, then spread it carefully, trying not to disturb the cake mixture underneath. Scatter over the almonds, followed by the pearl sugar.

* Bake for about 20 minutes, until the uncoated cake is well risen, firm to the touch, and coming away from the edge of the tin. Leave the topped cake in the oven for 5–10 minutes longer, until the topping is golden brown all over. It may still be moist and sticky underneath the crunchy surface, so check that a skewer inserted into the centre comes out clean.

* Leave to cool in the tins for 10 minutes before turning out on to a wire rack to cool completely. You should be able to get the topped cake clear of its tin and lining without turning it over and risking cracking the crust.

* To make the filling, mix the orange curd with the sifted icing sugar. You may need to add more curd or icing sugar to get a consistency like buttercream. Use the filling to sandwich the cakes together.

Fraisier

CLAIRE MELVIN

I recommend setting aside some 'me time' for this fabulous classic French cake with its crème mousseline filling and marzipan topping. You are bound to want it all to yourself! The strawberries run all the way through and provide a striking effect. Because of the dairy, this is best eaten chilled on the day it is made. Store in the fridge until just before serving.

SERVES 12–15

3 eggs

100g caster sugar

100g self-raising flour

4 tsp kirsch or crème de framboise

500–600g strawberries (reserve a large one to decorate the top of the cake)

Crème Mousseline:

6 eggs

240g caster sugar

50g plain flour

500ml semi-skimmed milk

250g butter, at room temperature

2 tsp kirsch or crème de framboise

a few drops of vanilla extract

Decoration:

pink food colouring

200g marzipan

✳ Preheat the oven to 180°C/fan 160°C/gas mark 4. Grease and line a 23cm round, springform cake tin.

✳ Whisk the eggs and sugar in a large bowl using an electric whisk until they are very pale and have doubled in volume. Sift over a third of the flour and fold in gently using a large metal spoon, being careful not to knock out the air. Fold in the remaining flour in two batches.

✳ Carefully transfer the mixture to the tin, spreading it evenly. Bake for 20–25 minutes, until golden brown and springy to the touch. Leave to cool in the tin for a few minutes, before turning out on to a wire rack to cool completely.

✳ For the crème mouselline, firstly make a crème patissière by putting the eggs, sugar, flour and 200ml of the milk in a saucepan and heating gently, stirring continuously, until it comes to a simmer.

✳ Keep stirring until it is thickened and smooth, then gradually stir in the remaining milk. Simmer very gently for about 3 minutes. Dice half the butter and stir it in a few pieces at a time until melted and smooth. Remove from the heat, press a piece of cling film over the surface to prevent a skin forming, and leave to cool.

✳ Put the remaining butter into a large bowl and beat with an electric mixer until very soft and creamy. Gradually beat in the cooled pastry cream until you have a smooth, light mixture. Beat in the kirsch and vanilla, then chill.

CONTINUED ▸

✳ To assemble, cut the sponge in half horizontally using a large serrated knife. Put one half into the cake tin you used earlier and brush all over with kirsch. Using a palette knife, spread a thin layer of crème mousseline over this sponge. Cut about 12–14 strawberries in half lengthways and place these around the edge of the cake, cut sides touching the tin, points upwards. Fill the centre with whole strawberries, points upwards. Spread enough of the crème mousseline on top to cover the strawberries and fill the gaps.

✳ Brush the second sponge layer all over with kirsch, then place on top and press down gently. Remove the cake from the tin and cover the top and sides of the second sponge with the remaining crème mousseline.

✳ To finish, knead a little pink colouring into the marzipan until you have an even colour. On a surface dusted with icing sugar, roll out the marzipan to 3mm thick. Cut out a 23cm circle, place on top of the cake and smooth out. Decorate the top of the cake with a sliced, fanned strawberry. Put the cake in the fridge for at least half an hour before serving.

Tia Maria & Mascarpone Cake

HELEN JONES

Here's a cakey twist on tiramisu! Bake it a day in advance and brush the sponge with the syrup, then leave overnight to let the flavours mingle. For extra clout, pour another drop or two of Tia Maria over the sponge just before assembling, allowing it to soak through before finishing off. You may as well pour another dash into a glass and add some ice, to enjoy with a slice of this cake! See photo overleaf.

SERVES 12

200g butter, softened
200g caster sugar
4 eggs
200g self-raising flour

Tia Maria Syrup:
85g caster sugar
50ml Tia Maria

Cream Filling:
1 x 284ml carton of
    double cream
250g mascarpone
3 tbsp caster sugar
cocoa powder, to dust

* Preheat the oven to 190°C/fan 170°C/gas mark 5. Butter two 20cm round sandwich tins and line each with a circle of baking parchment.

* Beat the butter and sugar using a wooden spoon or electric mixer until light and fluffy. Add the eggs one at a time, beating well after each addition, and adding a tablespoon of the flour with the final egg to help prevent curdling.

* Sift in the remaining flour and fold in using a large metal spoon until the flour is just combined. Carefully pour the mixture into the tins, spreading it evenly. Bake for about 20 minutes, then turn out on to a wire rack to cool.

* For the syrup, place the sugar, Tia Maria and two tablespoons of water in a small saucepan and heat gently, until the sugar has dissolved. Cut each cooled cake in half horizontally using a large serrated knife and brush the syrup all over the four pieces of cake.

* Make the filling. Whip the cream until soft peaks form. In a large bowl, beat the mascarpone and caster sugar to loosen the cheese, then fold in the cream and mix until smooth.

* To assemble, spoon a third of the cream filling over one of the cake halves. Sift some cocoa powder over the filling, then cover with another cake layer. Repeat this twice more then lay the final cake on top. Dust the top with cocoa powder. This cake is best eaten chilled – place in the fridge for an hour before serving.

Irish Coffee Cake

WITH BAILEYS FROSTING

GARY MORTON

Coffee cake is such a popular tearoom favourite. Here, Gary has given it a bit of delicious Irish booziness by adding a Baileys cream cheese frosting. Topped with grated dark chocolate, it's the perfect afternoon or after-dinner treat.

SERVES 10–12

250g butter, softened

250g caster sugar

4 large eggs

250g self-raising flour

2 tbsp coffee extract or essence

50g good-quality dark chocolate, to decorate

Baileys Frosting:

200g butter, softened

400g full-fat cream cheese

200g icing sugar

2 tbsp Baileys

✴ Preheat the oven to 180°C/fan 160°C/gas mark 4. Grease and line two 20cm round sandwich tins.

✴ Beat the butter and sugar using a wooden spoon or electric mixer until light and fluffy. Add the eggs one at a time, beating well after each addition, and adding a tablespoon of the flour with the final egg to help prevent curdling. Sift in the remaining flour and beat to combine, then add the coffee extract.

✴ Divide the mixture between the tins, spreading it evenly. Bake for 20–25 minutes, until a skewer inserted into the centre comes out clean. Turn out on to a wire rack and leave to cool completely.

✴ Meanwhile, make the frosting. Beat the butter until smooth. Add the cream cheese and mix until combined, then sift in the icing sugar and beat until light and fluffy. Mix in the Baileys. If the frosting is too soft, chill it briefly to firm up a little.

✴ Sandwich the cakes together with some of the frosting then use the remainder to cover the top and sides of the whole cake. Grate the chocolate over the top to decorate.

Choo Choo Chai Cake

JANET CURRIE

The inspiration for this recipe came from a Clandestine event held in a charming vintage tearoom on the Great Central Railway, where Janet was wowed by a 'three milks' cake. A great fan of chai, the aromatic spiced tea, she incorporated the flavour, creating a deliciously moist cake with a fragrant mix of spices and syrup. The cake freezes well without the topping.

SERVES 8–10

200g butter, softened
200g caster sugar
4 eggs
200ml soured cream
1 tsp vanilla extract,
    or the scraped seeds
    of ½ a vanilla pod
200g self-raising flour
2 tsp ground cinnamon, plus
    extra to dust (optional)
1 tsp ground ginger
½ tsp freshly grated nutmeg
1 tsp ground cloves
1 tsp ground cardamom
½ tsp bicarbonate of soda

Soaking Milk:
200ml double cream
200ml sweetened
    condensed milk
100ml evaporated milk
100ml chai syrup (or use
    4 tbsp caster sugar
    mixed with 4 tbsp
    strong chai tea)

Topping (optional):
250ml whipping cream
1 tbsp icing sugar
½ tsp vanilla extract

* Preheat the oven to 180°C/fan 160°C/gas mark 4. Grease and line a 23cm round, loose-bottomed cake tin.

* Beat the butter and sugar using a wooden spoon or electric mixer until light and fluffy. Add two of the eggs and half the soured cream, beating well to combine, then add the other two eggs and remaining soured cream, then the vanilla.

* In a separate bowl, mix the flour, spices and bicarbonate of soda. Sift over the cake mixture and fold in gently until thoroughly combined. Transfer the mixture to the tin, spreading it evenly. Bake for about 40 minutes or until a skewer inserted into the centre comes out clean. Leave in the tin to cool.

* When the cake is completely cool prick the surface all over with a fork. Wrap the base of the tin in cling film so that it is liquid proof. Mix the cream, milks and chai syrup in a jug, then pour over the cake and place in the fridge for at least 4 hours or overnight.

* Turn the cake out on to a serving plate with a rim (to stop any liquid escaping onto the table), reserving any of the milk and syrup mixture that hasn't soaked in.

* If you want to add a topping to the cake, whip the cream, sugar and vanilla until stiff peaks form, then spread on top of the cake. Lightly dust with cinnamon, if you like, and serve with a drizzle of the reserved soaking liquid.

Citrus fruits make for the most
mouth-watering and zingy cakes.
Their zesty flavours go well with so many
other ingredients, from chocolate to coconut
and many others in between. It's hard not
to love a good lemon drizzle, but our club
members like to take things a little bit further
and add their own stamp to the citrus theme.
One of the Clandestine bakers has even
experimented with lemon and parsnip!
It may sound like an odd combination but
it's delicious. These cakes make a great
centrepiece for spring and summer with their
bold, bright, fresh flavours, but they will
bring a little sunshine into your life
at any time of year.

Zesty
Cakes

Lime & Coconut Drizzle Loaf

JOANNA MYERS

The secret to this tropical drizzle cake is to add the syrup at 10-minute intervals to allow the cake to soak up all the delicious zingy flavours. The addition of Malibu is a boozy, coconutty bonus. Fit for an island paradise!

SERVES 10–12

100g desiccated coconut,
    plus 1–2 tbsp to decorate
3 tbsp Malibu
225g butter, very soft
225g caster sugar
275g self-raising flour
2 tsp baking powder
4 eggs
4 tbsp milk
finely grated zest of 3 limes

Malibu Topping:
2 tbsp Malibu
juice of 3 limes
120g caster sugar

* Preheat the oven to 160°C/fan 140°C/gas mark 3. Grease and line a 900g loaf tin.

* Soak the coconut in the Malibu while you get on with making the cake – this will soften the coconut and increase the strength of its flavour in the finished cake. Put all the remaining cake ingredients into a large bowl and beat until smooth and of a dropping consistency. Add the coconut and mix until well combined.

* Pour the mixture into the tin, spreading it evenly and smoothing the top. Bake for 1¼–1½ hours or until well risen and springy to the touch and a skewer inserted into the centre comes out clean. Leave to cool slightly in the tin.

* For the topping, combine the Malibu, lime juice and sugar in a small bowl to make a runny syrup. When the cake has cooled slightly, liberally brush the syrup on to the top of the cake. Do this several times, roughly at 10-minute intervals. This allows the drizzle to soak into the cake. Be careful not to oversoak the cake – you may not need all of the syrup.

* Decorate the cake by sprinkling the extra coconut over the top after the final drizzle. Leave the cake to cool completely before lifting out of the tin with the aid of the baking paper. Remove the paper to serve.

Crispy Lemon Cake

JULIANA MORRIS

This tried-and-tested recipe was discovered in a cookery binder that Juliana inherited from her nan. The sponge is drizzled with a lemony syrup that sets into a crispy, crunchy topping. It's very easy to make, so is a great cake to try if you are new to baking. You can also make it with lime zest and a lime syrup for a sharper version.

SERVES 12

225g butter, softened
340g caster sugar
4 eggs
340g self-raising flour
grated zest and juice
    of 2 lemons
½ tsp baking powder
120ml milk

Crispy Topping:
225g caster sugar
juice of 2 lemons, plus a little
    grated zest to decorate

* Preheat the oven to 160°C/fan 140°C/gas mark 3. Grease and line a 20cm round, springform cake tin.

* Beat the butter and sugar using a wooden spoon or electric mixer until light and fluffy. Add the eggs one at a time, beating well after each addition, and adding a tablespoon of the flour with the final egg to help prevent curdling. Add the lemon zest and juice, then sift in the remaining flour and baking powder and fold in until thoroughly combined, then mix in the milk.

* Spoon the mixture into the tin, spreading it evenly. Bake for about 1 hour or until risen and golden brown.

* Meanwhile, prepare the topping. Mix the sugar and lemon juice to make a sugary lemony sauce – much like you would have on pancakes.

* When the cake comes out of the oven, prick all over with a skewer, then drizzle with the lemon topping and leave in the tin to cool completely before turning out. Decorate the top with a few sprinkles of lemon zest.

Yoghurt, Lemon & Lime Cake

KATE DICKENS

'This cake will make you friends,' says Clandestine baker Kate, who brought this recipe to the UK with her all the way from New Zealand. She bakes it whenever she wants to break the ice with new people, and as she moves around a lot, it has made her friends in three different countries so far. Using a mild-tasting oil is essential so as not to overpower the sharp citrus notes and cool yoghurt taste.

SERVES 12–16

375g self-raising flour
500g caster sugar
grated zest of 2 lemons
grated zest of 1 lime
250ml natural yoghurt
250ml mild oil, such as
  sunflower or vegetable
  (not olive)
2 large eggs
icing sugar, to dust

Citrus Syrup:
juice of 2 lemons
juice of 1 lime
3 tbsp caster sugar

> TIP
> If you don't have a bundt tin, this can be made in a deep 23cm round tin. It may need a slightly shorter baking time, so check frequently until a skewer comes out clean.

* Preheat the oven to 190°C/fan 170°C/gas mark 5. Grease and flour a 2.5–3-litre bundt tin.

* Sift together the flour, sugar and citrus zests. In a separate bowl or jug beat together the yoghurt, oil and eggs.

* Mix the wet and dry mixtures together and transfer to the tin, spreading the batter out evenly. Bake for 45–50 minutes, until the cake is well risen and golden and a skewer inserted into the centre comes out clean.

* Meanwhile, make the lemon and lime syrup. Place the lemon and lime juice and the sugar in a small pan. Stir over a medium heat until the sugar is dissolved.

* As soon as the cake comes out of the oven, pierce it all over with a skewer, then spoon over the syrup, letting it soak into the cake between additions. Leave in the tin for 15–20 minutes, then turn the cake out on to a wire rack and leave to cool completely.

* Dust with icing sugar and present to prospective friends!

Syrupy Lemon Polenta Cake

RACHEL WHITE

Polenta is a great addition to cakes – it produces a lovely grainy texture and is also an excellent gluten-free alternative for anyone who needs to steer clear of flour. If ever there were an easy cake to bake it is this one! Be as generous as you like with the hot syrup and your cake will be even more moist. It's delicious served with crème fraîche.

SERVES 14–16

300g butter, softened
300g caster sugar
300g ground almonds
150g polenta
finely grated zest of 2 lemons
5 large eggs
icing sugar, to dust (optional)

Lemon Syrup:

juice of 1 lemon
2 tbsp icing sugar

* Preheat the oven to 180°C/fan 160°C/gas mark 4. Grease and line a 25cm round, loose-bottomed cake tin.

* Beat the butter and sugar using a wooden spoon or electric mixer until light and fluffy. Add the ground almonds, polenta and lemon zest and beat until combined. Add the eggs one at a time, beating well, until smooth. Transfer the mixture to the tin and spread evenly.

* Bake for about 50 minutes or until golden and firm to the touch. Leave in the tin for a few minutes, then turn out, upside down, on to a wire rack. Prick the base all over using a skewer or fork.

* To make the syrup, heat the lemon and icing sugar until boiling, then remove from the heat and spoon over the cake. Once the syrup has soaked in, you can either turn the cake the right way up or leave it as it is. Dust with icing sugar, if you wish.

Vegan Lemon Cake

LYNN HILL

You needn't be vegan to enjoy this light-textured, easy-to-bake cake with its sweet, zingy filling (though non-vegans might prefer to use real butter for a more indulgent frosting). The recipe can be easily adapted with other citrus fruits, such as oranges or limes, or you can replace the lemon juice with Cointreau for a boozy alternative. See photo on page 136.

SERVES 6–8

275g self-raising flour
200g caster sugar
1 tsp baking powder
3 tsp grated lemon zest
100ml corn oil
1 tbsp lemon juice or
   limoncello
icing sugar, to dust
slice of lemon, to decorate

Limoncello Filling:
100g soya margarine
300g icing sugar, sifted
2 tbsp limoncello

* Preheat the oven to 200°C/fan 180°C/gas mark 6. Brush two 20cm round sandwich tins with oil and line the bases with baking parchment.

* Place the flour, sugar, baking powder and lemon zest in a bowl and stir to mix. Add the oil, lemon juice or limoncello and 200ml cold water and beat until thoroughly combined.

* Divide the mixture between the tins, spreading it evenly. Bake for about 20 minutes or until a skewer inserted into the centre comes out clean. Leave to cool in the tins for a few minutes, then turn out on to a wire rack to cool completely.

* For the limoncello filling, place the margarine in a bowl and gradually beat in the icing sugar. Stir in the limoncello and beat until well combined.

* To assemble the cake, spread the filling over the top of one of the cooled sponges, then cover with the other sponge. Dust the top of the cake with icing sugar and decorate with the lemon slice.

Coconut Sunshine Cake

JINI MULUKUTLA

This rich, tropical cake will bring sunshine to your table with its crown of tangy orange icing and jewel-like covering of passion fruit seeds. For a simpler but no less stunning finish, you can sandwich the cake with raspberry jam and replace the passion fruit with a sprinkling of coconut. See photo on page 137.

SERVES 12–16

200g butter, softened
225g caster sugar
4 large eggs
225g self-raising flour
150ml coconut cream
1 tsp baking powder
pinch of salt
75g desiccated coconut
1–2 ripe, wrinkled
   passion fruit, to decorate

Orange Buttercream:
300g butter, softened
450g icing sugar
2 tbsp orange curd

* Preheat the oven to 180°C/fan 160°C/gas mark 4. Grease and line a 20cm round, springform cake tin.

* Beat the butter and sugar using a wooden spoon or electric mixer until light and fluffy. Add the eggs one at a time, beating well after each addition, and adding a tablespoon of the flour with the final egg to help prevent curdling. Whisk in the coconut cream, then fold in the remaining flour, baking powder, salt and desiccated coconut.

* Pour the mixture into the tin and spread out evenly. Bake the cake for 40–45 minutes or until a skewer inserted into the centre comes out clean. Leave to cool in the tin for a few minutes before turning out on to a wire rack to cool completely.

* Meanwhile, make the buttercream. Beat the butter with an electric mixer until light and fluffy, then gradually sift in the icing sugar and beat it in. Beat in the orange curd, then taste and add a little more if needed, but don't allow it to become too soft; the buttercream should be stiff enough to hold its shape.

* To assemble the cake, cut it in half horizontally and fill the middle with a layer of buttercream, then spread a smooth layer over the top of the cake. Fill a piping bag fitted with a star nozzle with the remaining buttercream and pipe rosettes around the top edge of the cake to form a crown.

* Cut the passion fruit in half and scoop out the flesh with a spoon, placing it on top of the cake. Gently spread with the back of the spoon. Refrigerate the cake for 30–60 minutes before serving to stop the icing from slipping.

VEGAN LEMON CAKE

LEMONY LEMONADE CAKE

COCONUT SUNSHINE CAKE

LEMON, PARSNIP & HAZELNUT CAKE

Lemony Lemonade Cake

ROB MARTIN

A fantastic way to use up leftover lemonade, this droolsome, almost pudding-like cake is perfect for a party. Children love it too. If you're feeling playful, decorate the top with gummy sweets. See photo on page 136.

SERVES 8–10

200g plain flour
250g caster sugar
½ tsp bicarbonate of soda
¼ tsp salt
1 egg
125ml buttermilk
finely grated zest of 2 lemons,
    plus 2 tbsp juice
125g butter
150ml lemonade

Icing:
25g butter
25ml lemonade
2 tbsp lemon juice
225g icing sugar

✳ Preheat the oven to 180°C/fan 160°C/gas mark 4. Grease and line a 23cm round, springform cake tin.

✳ Place the flour, sugar, bicarbonate of soda and salt in a bowl and mix. In a separate bowl or jug, beat the egg, buttermilk, lemon zest and juice.

✳ Place the butter and lemonade in a saucepan and heat gently until the butter has melted. Remove from the heat, pour over the dry ingredients and mix well. Add the egg and buttermilk mixture and beat until everything is thoroughly combined. The batter will be very runny.

✳ Pour the mixture into the tin, spreading it evenly. Bake for 40 minutes or until a skewer inserted into the centre comes out clean.

✳ Leave to cool in the tin for about 15 minutes (it should still be warm when you ice it), then turn out on to a wire rack set over a baking sheet (this will catch any icing that runs off the cake).

✳ To make the icing, place the butter and lemonade in a small saucepan and stir over a low heat until the butter has melted, then remove from the heat. Add the lemon juice, then gradually sift in the icing sugar until you have a smooth pouring consistency. Pour the icing over the still warm cake, and leave to cool and set before serving.

Lemon, Parsnip & Hazelnut Cake

GILLIAN TARRY

Parsnip might sound like a rather unconventional cake ingredient, but you really must give it a try! As with carrots in carrot cake, parsnip adds a delicate, subtle sweetness and creates a sponge that is moist and stays that way for days. You can experiment with other grated vegetables as an alternative, but make sure you squeeze any excess moisture from them before adding to the batter. See photo on page 137.

SERVES 8–10

350g parsnips, peeled and grated (squeeze out any moisture)

finely grated zest of 3 lemons

250ml rapeseed oil

3 large eggs

85g roasted hazelnuts, chopped, plus 25g chopped, to decorate

125g stem ginger, chopped

250g self-raising flour

175g soft light brown sugar

Lemon Cream Cheese Frosting:

125g butter

250g full-fat cream cheese

2 tbsp lemon juice

125g icing sugar

✳ Preheat the oven to 190°C/fan 170°C/gas mark 5. Grease and line two 20cm round sandwich tins.

✳ In a large bowl, combine the parsnips, lemon zest, oil, eggs, hazelnuts and stem ginger, then add the flour and sugar. Mix well.

✳ Spoon the mixture into the tins, spreading it evenly. Bake for about 30 minutes or until a skewer inserted into the centre comes out clean. Turn out on to a wire rack to cool completely.

✳ To make the frosting, beat the butter until smooth, then add the cream cheese and lemon juice and mix until combined. Finally sift in the icing sugar and beat until light and fluffy.

✳ To assemble the cake, place one of the cooled sponges on a serving plate and spread a third of the frosting over the top. Place the other sponge on top, then use the remaining frosting to cover the top and sides of the whole cake. Decorate with the extra chopped hazelnuts.

Bake me,
I'm yours!

Pistachio & Lime Cake

LYNN HILL

This beautiful cake is a pistachio-flavoured sponge soaked in a zesty lime syrup and layered with a lime cream cheese frosting, lime curd and crunchy pistachio nuts. It has endless texture and tang. Go to town with the decoration and you'll have yourself a cake fit for a cookbook cover! See also photos overleaf and on front cover.

SERVES 10–12

300g butter, softened

300g caster sugar

5 eggs

300g self-raising flour

1 tsp baking powder

grated zest of 3 limes, plus the juice of 2

50g pistachio nuts, finely chopped

Lime Syrup:

juice of 2 limes

2 tbsp caster sugar

Lime Curd:

60g butter, diced

2 eggs

170g caster sugar

grated zest and juice of 3 limes

Frosting & Decoration:

250g butter, softened

200g full-fat cream cheese, from the fridge

grated zest of 1 lime

250g icing sugar

75g good-quality dark chocolate (min. 70% cocoa solids)

125g pistachio nuts, chopped

a few unsprayed rose petals (optional)

＊ Preheat the oven to 190°C/fan 170°C/gas mark 5. Grease and line three 20cm round sandwich tins.

＊ Beat the butter and sugar using a wooden spoon or electric mixer until light and fluffy. Add the eggs one at a time, beating well after each addition, and adding a tablespoon of the flour with the final egg to help prevent curdling.

＊ Fold in the remaining flour and the baking powder until thoroughly combined. Add the lime zest and juice and the finely chopped pistachio nuts and mix until well combined.

＊ Divide the mixture between the tins, spreading it evenly. Bake for 25–30 minutes or until a skewer inserted into the centre comes out clean. Leave in the tins to cool slightly.

＊ Meanwhile, make the syrup. Put the lime juice and sugar into a pan over a low heat and stir until the sugar has completely dissolved, then bring to a simmer. Remove from the heat and leave to cool.

＊ While the sponges are still warm turn them out of their tins on to a wire rack, then carefully spoon the lime syrup over the top of each one – you may not need all the syrup. Leave the cakes to cool completely.

＊ Put all the ingredients for the lime curd in a small, heavy-based pan and heat gently, stirring constantly with a wooden spoon – don't let the mixture boil or the eggs will scramble. When it has thickened enough to coat the back of the spoon quite thickly, strain through a sieve into a bowl. Cover and leave to cool.

＊ To make the frosting, beat the butter until smooth. Add the cream cheese and mix until combined. Add the lime zest, then sift in the icing sugar and beat until light and fluffy.

CONTINUED ➡

Pistachio & Lime Cake

✳ For the decoration, melt the chocolate in a bowl set over a pan of gently simmering water, making sure the water does not touch the base of the bowl, then pour it on to a piece of baking parchment and spread it out with a palette knife so it is about 3mm thick. Scatter over some of the chopped pistachios and leave to cool and set.

✳ To assemble the cake, place one of the cooled cakes on a plate, spread with a third of the frosting, then cover with a generous layer of the lime curd. Add a sprinkling of the remaining chopped pistachio nuts. Place a second cake on top of this and repeat the layers (saving some pistachios for the top). Place the final cake on top and cover with the remaining frosting.

✳ Break the pistachio-studded chocolate into rough shards and arrange round the edge of the top of the cake, then scatter the remaining pistachios among them. Decorate the centre with a few rose petals, if you like.

Citrus Sunbeam Layer Cake
WITH LIMONCELLO FROSTING

LYNN HILL

The sun will certainly be shining as you cut yourself a slice of this impressive stripy orange and lemon extravaganza! Its sweet cream cheese frosting is laced with limoncello for extra indulgence. Don't panic if you don't own six cake tins – you can easily bake the layers in batches, just remember to allow yourself a bit of extra time.

SERVES 16–20

400g butter, softened
400g caster sugar
6 large eggs
400g self-raising flour, sifted
grated zest of 2 lemons
    and 2 oranges
yellow and orange liquid
    food colourings
2 tbsp milk (optional)

Citrus Syrups:

juice of 1 lemon and
    1 orange
1 tbsp limoncello
50g caster sugar

Frosting:

125g butter, softened
250g full-fat cream cheese,
    from the fridge
500g icing sugar, sifted
1 tbsp limoncello

* Preheat the oven to 190°C/fan 170°C/gas mark 5. Grease and line six 20cm round sandwich tins.

* Beat the butter and sugar using a wooden spoon or electric mixer until light and fluffy. Beat the eggs in a jug and gently add to the creamed mixture, beating all the time and adding some of the flour to help prevent curdling. Fold in the remaining flour.

* Divide the mixture in half and add the lemon zest and a tablespoon of yellow colouring to one half and the orange zest and a tablespoon of orange colouring to the other half. (Liquid colouring does help loosen the batter somewhat, so if you are using powder or paste colour, add a tablespoon of milk to each half to achieve the equivalent consistency.)

* Divide the mixture between the tins, spreading it evenly. Or bake the layers individually or in batches if you have fewer tins. You need three lemon layers and three orange layers.

* Bake in the oven for 10 minutes or until a skewer inserted into the centre comes out clean. Don't overbake or the cake will be dry. Leave to cool in the tins for a few minutes then turn out on to baking paper set on a wire rack to cool completely.

* While the cake layers are cooling, make the syrups. Combine the lemon juice with the limoncello and half the caster sugar. Heat gently in a pan until the sugar has dissolved, then bring to a simmer and remove from the heat. In another pan combine the orange juice with the remaining sugar. Heat gently until the sugar has dissolved, then bring to a simmer and remove from the heat. Transfer the syrups to individual bowls and set aside to cool.

CONTINUED ➤

✳ While the syrups are cooling, make the frosting. Beat the butter then add the cream cheese and beat until smooth. Gradually sift in the icing sugar and beat until the mixture is light and fluffy. Add the limoncello for a touch of decadence and the frosting is complete. Place in the fridge for a few moments to firm up if it's a little runny or add a little more sifted icing sugar if very runny.

✳ To assemble, place an orange cake layer on to your favourite plate or cake stand and brush with some of the orange syrup but do not oversoak. Cover with a thin layer of the frosting, then repeat with the remaining sponges, alternating the lemon and orange layers.

✳ Finally, cover the top and sides of the whole cake with the remaining frosting. Decorate with a little orange and lemon zest, if you wish.

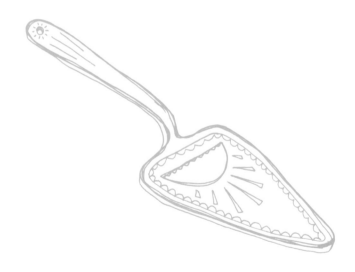

Ricotta & Lemon Sponge Cake

LYNN HILL

I make no apologies for the indulgent filling here: some cakes have more than their fair share of deliciousness and this is one of them. The sponge itself is light and fresh and lets the filling take centre stage with the lovely texture of ricotta and the distinctive limoncello taste. It really packs a punch. For a summer treat, serve in the garden with a glass of iced limoncello on the side. See photo overleaf.

SERVES 8–10

200g butter, softened
200g caster sugar
3 large eggs
200g self-raising flour
grated zest of 2 lemons,
 plus 1 tbsp juice

Lemon Syrup:
juice of 2 lemons
2 tsp caster sugar

Ricotta & Limoncello Filling:
80g butter, softened
160g full-fat cream
 cheese, from the fridge
160g ricotta cheese,
 from the fridge
50g icing sugar, sifted
1 tsp limoncello
grated zest of 1 lemon
1 tsp lemon juice

✳ Preheat the oven to 190°C/fan 170°C/gas mark 5. Grease and line two 20cm round sandwich tins.

✳ Beat the butter and sugar using a wooden spoon or electric mixer until light and fluffy. Add the eggs one at a time, beating well after each addition, and adding a tablespoon of the flour with the final egg to help prevent curdling. Fold in the remaining flour until thoroughly combined, then add the lemon zest and juice.

✳ Divide the mixture between the tins, spreading it evenly. Bake for about 20 minutes, until a skewer inserted into the centre comes out clean. Turn out on to a wire rack to cool.

✳ Make the lemon syrup. Place the lemon juice and caster sugar in a small pan and heat gently until the sugar has dissolved, then bring to a simmer. Remove from the heat and leave to cool a little before spooning over both sponges while they are still warm (but not straight out of the oven).

✳ To make the filling, beat the butter in a bowl until smooth. Add the cream cheese and mix until combined, then add the ricotta and finally the sifted icing sugar and beat until thoroughly combined. The mixture may look a little grainy but that is because of the texture of the ricotta. Add the limoncello, lemon zest and juice and mix until well combined. Place the filling in the fridge to firm up.

✳ When the soaked sponges are completely cool, remove the filling from the fridge and use the whole amount to cover the top of one of the sponges; top with the second sponge, then dust the top of the cake with icing sugar.

Ricotta & Lemon Sponge Cake

Lemon & Poppy Seed Cake

Lemon Meringue Cake

Lemon Meringue Cake

LYNN HILL

Inspired by lemon meringue pie, this cake has a zesty middle and a crisp meringue top. Be really generous with the lemon zest (in my household, any leftover lemons are always welcome in a G & T!). A good-quality lemon curd is essential if you want that cheek-sucking tangy citrus taste. Try varying the recipe with a different curd, such as lime or even rhubarb!

SERVES 8–10

200g butter, softened
200g caster sugar
3 eggs, lightly beaten
250g self-raising flour
2 tbsp lemon curd
3–4 tbsp milk

Meringue:
3 egg whites
170g caster sugar

Filling:
115g butter, softened
170g full-fat cream cheese, from the fridge
55g icing sugar
grated zest of 1 large lemon
about 300g good-quality lemon curd

* Preheat the oven to 180°C/fan 160°C/gas mark 4. Grease and line two 20cm round sandwich tins.

* Beat the butter and sugar using a wooden spoon or electric mixer until light and fluffy. Add the eggs one at a time, beating well after each addition, and adding a tablespoon of the flour with the final egg to prevent curdling. Add the lemon curd, then fold in the remaining flour until well combined. Add enough of the milk to reach a dropping consistency.

* Divide the mixture between the tins, spreading it evenly. Bake in the oven for 20 minutes until slightly golden and almost done and a skewer inserted into the centre comes out clean.

* Meanwhile, make the meringue. In a scrupulously clean bowl, whisk the egg whites until stiff then whisk in half the sugar, a tablespoonful at a time. Fold in the remaining sugar.

* Remove the sponges from the oven, then spread just under half the meringue over one of them, smoothing the top – try to prevent it touching the sides of the tin, otherwise it will be difficult to turn out.

* Put the remaining meringue on the other cake and swirl into peaks (this will be the top sponge). Return the cakes to the oven for about 10 minutes, until the meringue is crisp and pale golden. Remove from the oven and leave to cool in the tin for a few minutes before turning out on to a wire rack to cool completely.

* To make the filling, beat the butter then add the cream cheese and beat until smooth. Gradually sift in the icing sugar and beat until the mixture is light and fluffy but not runny. Add the lemon zest and two tablespoons of the lemon curd. Gently spread the filling over the sponge with the flat meringue top, then cover the filling with the remaining lemon curd and top with the other sponge.

Lemon & Poppy Seed Cake

RACHEL MCGRATH

This is a substantial cake with an impressively zingy taste and fluffy texture. If you want to try a different flavour, replace the poppy seeds with two tablespoons of chopped thyme. It will keep for up to three days in an airtight container. See photo on page 148.

SERVES 12

225g butter, softened
450g golden caster sugar
6 eggs
420g plain flour
½ tsp bicarbonate of soda
1 tsp ground ginger
½ tsp salt
20g poppy seeds
1 tsp lemon extract
250ml natural yoghurt
juice and zest of 2 large
    lemons

Lemon Glaze:
juice of 1 lemon
150g icing sugar

* Preheat the oven to 190°C/fan 170°C/gas mark 5. Grease and flour a 2.5–3-litre bundt tin.

* Beat the butter and sugar using a wooden spoon or electric mixer until light and fluffy. Add the eggs one at a time, beating well after each addition, and adding a tablespoon of the flour with the final egg to help prevent curdling.

* Sift the remaining flour, and the bicarbonate of soda, ginger and salt into a separate bowl and stir in the poppy seeds. Combine the lemon extract, yoghurt, lemon juice and zest in a jug.

* Add a third of the flour mixture to the egg mixture and mix until just incorporated. Add half the yoghurt mixture and mix until just incorporated. Repeat in the same proportions until all the mixtures have been combined. If using a mixer, give the batter a final blast on a slow setting for about 15 seconds; if not, mix carefully with a wooden spoon. This makes sure everything is combined without overworking the flour.

* Pour the batter into the tin; if it's a decorative tin, make sure you push it into all the grooves. Bake in the oven for 50 minutes–1 hour or until a skewer inserted into the centre comes out clean. The cake will be shrinking away from the sides ever so slightly. Leave in the tin to cool completely.

* To make the glaze, add enough lemon juice to the icing sugar to form a runny icing. Drizzle over the cooled cake.

Grapefruit Loaf

ANN JENNINGS

Lower in fat and sugar than most cakes, this is a healthier option but one that tastes good too. Grapefruit fans will love its sharpness, while those with a sweeter tooth might prefer to swap the grapefruit for mandarin segments, which are also more likely to appeal to children. Don't be concerned if the batter seems very loose – this is normal, as is the fairly dense texture of the finished cake.

SERVES 8

50g sultanas

½ x 540g can grapefruit segments in juice, roughly chopped (reserve the juice)

50g butter, softened

50g caster sugar

50g self-raising flour

1 tsp baking powder

50g oats

2 eggs, lightly beaten

* The night before or several hours in advance place the sultanas in a dish. Cover with the grapefruit segments and their juice and leave in the fridge to soak.

* Preheat the oven to 200°C/fan 180°C/gas mark 6. Grease and line a 500g loaf tin.

* Drain the sultanas and grapefruit through a sieve placed over a bowl, pressing gently with the back of a spoon to remove excess juice. Transfer the juice to a small pan and set aside; reserve the fruit.

* Put the butter, sugar, flour, baking powder and oats into a food processor and add most of the beaten eggs. Process until smooth, adding the remainder of the beaten eggs, if necessary, to achieve a soft dropping consistency. Stir in the soaked fruit using a wooden spoon.

* Pour the mixture into the tin and bake for 40–45 minutes, until golden and a skewer inserted into the centre comes out clean.

* Bring the reserved soaking liquid to the boil and boil rapidly until you have a thick glaze – you will need about two tablespoons. Remove the glaze from the heat and brush over the loaf with a pastry brush. Turn the cake out on to a wire rack and leave to cool completely.

Orange & White Chocolate Cake

LYNN HILL

This delicious orangey syrup-soaked cake has a moreish white chocolate filling. Use a premium chocolate and ensure that it has cooled completely before adding to your buttercream, or it will separate and you will have to start all over again. Don't say I didn't warn you!

SERVES 8–10

225g butter, softened
225g caster sugar
4 large eggs, beaten
225g self-raising flour
zest of 1 large orange
½ tsp baking powder
1 tbsp milk (optional)
icing sugar, to dust
orange slice, to decorate

Orange Syrup:

grated zest and juice of
    1 large orange
1 tsp orange blossom water
    or 2 tsp Cointreau
1 tsp caster sugar

White Chocolate Filling:

150g white chocolate,
    broken into chunks
grated zest of 2 large oranges,
    plus 4 tbsp juice
200g butter, softened
75g icing sugar

TIPS

If the filling is loose after beating, leave it in the fridge for a few minutes. Leftover filling can be kept in the fridge for up to three days or frozen for up to a week. Defrost at room temperature before using.

* Preheat the oven to 190°C/fan 170°C/gas mark 5. Grease and line two 20cm round sandwich tins.

* Beat the butter and sugar until light and fluffy, then add the eggs gradually, beating well after each addition, and adding a tablespoon of the flour with the final addition to help prevent curdling. Mix in the orange zest, then fold in the remaining flour and the baking powder until thoroughly combined. If the mixture looks a little stiff add the milk to loosen it and reach a dropping consistency.

* Divide the mixture between the tins and bake for 20–25 minutes or until a skewer inserted into the centre comes out clean. Leave in the tins to cool slightly.

* Meanwhile, make the syrup. Put the orange zest and juice, orange blossom water (or Cointreau) and sugar into a pan over a low heat and stir until the sugar has completely dissolved, then bring to a simmer. Remove from the heat and leave to cool a little. Turn the cakes out of the tins on to a wire rack, then spoon the syrup over the two sponges but do not oversoak – you may not need all the syrup. Leave the cakes to cool completely.

* To make the chocolate filling, place the chocolate in a heatproof bowl. Put the orange zest and juice in a small saucepan and bring to a simmer. Simmer for a couple of minutes, then pour over the chocolate. Stir until thoroughly combined and the chocolate has completely melted. If it does not fully melt, set the bowl of chocolate mix over a pan of simmering water and stir gently. Set aside to cool completely.

* In a separate bowl, beat the butter and icing sugar until light and fluffy. Gradually add the cold chocolate, beating all the time, until thoroughly combined. (Be warned that if the chocolate mixture is still warm it will melt the butter and you will have to start all over again.)

* Sandwich the cooled cakes with the filling, then dust the top with icing sugar and decorate with a slice of orange to serve.

Blood Orange & Rosemary Cake

KATHY CREMIN

Blood oranges are much sharper than regular oranges and give this cake a spicy tartness. Be generous with the rosemary and the end result will be a gorgeous explosion of warm earthy flavours, with the ground cardamom adding a beautiful perfume. Kathy recommends buttering the insides of the lined tin and coating with fine polenta, which crisps up and caramelises around the edge of the cake.

SERVES 12

fine polenta, for coating
    the tin
200g ground almonds
    (or replace partially or
    wholly with polenta,
    as wished)
200g caster sugar
200ml olive oil
4 large eggs
pinch of sea salt
grated zest of 2 large lemons
grated zest of 2 blood oranges
1 scant tsp green cardamom
    seeds, finely ground
4 sprigs of rosemary,
    leaves only, finely chopped,
    or ground, if possible

Blood Orange &
Rosemary Syrup:

juice of 2 large lemons
juice of 2 blood oranges
    plus 1 whole blood orange,
    peeled, pith removed, thinly
    sliced
4 sprigs of rosemary
100–150g icing sugar

* Preheat the oven to 160°C/fan 140°C/gas mark 3. Grease and line a 900g loaf tin then grease the paper and coat the insides with polenta.

* In a large bowl, beat together all the cake ingredients until they are thoroughly combined. Pour the mixture into the tin, spreading it evenly. Bake in the oven for 45 minutes–1 hour or until the top is golden and springs back when gently pressed – be aware that this cake remains very moist when cooked.

* Meanwhile, make the syrup. Place the lemon juice, blood orange juice, rosemary sprigs and 50g of the icing sugar in a small pan and bring to a gentle simmer, stirring until the sugar dissolves and the liquid has reduced by half – don't let it boil. (It is best to start with just this 50g of icing sugar and up the amount to get the sweetness you desire. If you don't use much sugar, reduce the syrup further – you want to end up with a thick syrup.) Remove from the heat and set aside while the cake is baking.

* As soon as the cake comes out of the oven, prick the top all over with a skewer. Lift the rosemary sprigs out of the syrup then pour two-thirds of the still-warm syrup slowly over the cake to let it absorb.

* Cover the top of the cake with blood orange slices, then pour over the remaining syrup. Leave to cool in the tin to allow the syrup to soak in.

* This cake is very moist and should come easily out of the tin but once removed it won't transfer easily from plate to plate – to do this, cover with a plate, invert and tap the bottom. Once released, put the presentation plate on top and flip the whole thing the right way up again. Serve warm or cold, with blood orange segments and Greek yoghurt.

Dark 'n' Stormy Cake

ROB MARTIN

In honour of the cocktail of the same name, Rob created this zesty cake for one of the Clandestine Cake Club's primetime TV appearances, on The Alan Titchmarsh Show. *Despite the name, it's actually rather light and sunny. It certainly wowed viewers, and got a huge thumbs-up when served to the crew and audience after the show.*

SERVES 10–12

180g self-raising flour
1 tsp ground ginger
90g butter
6 eggs
180g caster sugar
100g crystallised ginger,
  finely chopped

Rum Syrup:
2 tbsp rum
65g granulated sugar

**Lime Cream Cheese
  Frosting:**
150g butter, softened
250g cream cheese
200g icing sugar, sifted
finely grated zest of 2 limes
lime juice, to taste

* Preheat the oven to 190°C/fan 170°C/gas mark 5. Grease and line two 20cm round sandwich tins.

* Sift the flour and ginger into a bowl. Melt the butter in a small saucepan and set aside to cool. Place the eggs and sugar in a large bowl and whisk using an electric hand whisk. Keep whisking until the mixture has tripled in volume and is very thick and creamy.

* Sift in a third of the flour mixture and fold in very gently with a metal spoon, then fold in the remaining flour in two batches. Pour the cooled melted butter in around the edge of the mixture, then add the crystallised ginger and fold them in carefully, trying not to knock out the air. Divide the mixture between the tins, spreading it evenly. Bake for about 20 minutes or until golden and firm.

* Meanwhile, for the syrup, gently heat the rum, sugar and one tablespoon of water until the sugar has dissolved. Do not let it boil.

* As soon as the sponges come out of the oven, prick each sponge all over with a skewer, then drizzle equal amounts of the syrup over each. Leave to cool in the tins for a few minutes before turning out on to a wire rack to cool completely.

* For the frosting, beat the butter until smooth. Add the cream cheese and mix until combined, then sift in the icing sugar and beat until light and fluffy. Finally add the lime zest and lime juice, to taste, being careful not to thin the frosting too much.

* To assemble the cake, cover the top of one sponge with a thin layer of frosting, top with the other sponge, then use the remaining frosting to cover the top and sides of the whole cake.

No baking book would be complete without
a chapter dedicated to chocolate. After all,
who doesn't love a good, rich, sinful slice?
Clandestine members find all manner of ways
to make this indulgent ingredient suit pretty
much any theme or variation, whether
it's milk, dark or white chocolate, used in
the sponge, filling or as decoration
(or even better, all of the above!).

As ever, club members don't just stick to
the traditional – we like to get inventive, so
here you'll find outrageously good recipes
that will make any chocoholic weep
with happiness.

Chocolatey Cakes

Dark Chocolate Nut Cake

SUE ARON

This rich, nutty cake reminds Sue of her childhood, when her mother used to make it each year for her birthday. One time, they placed the cake on a windowsill for the ganache to set, and upon their return the cake was decorated with a collection of little footprints and all the hazelnuts had disappeared... so this recipe comes with a warning to keep it well away from squirrels! Rich and nutty, without being cloying, it will keep really well in the fridge for 3–4 days if wrapped in foil.

SERVES 12

170g good-quality dark
   chocolate (min. 60%
   cocoa solids), broken up

170g butter, softened

170g icing sugar

6 eggs, separated

170g ground hazelnuts, plus
   extra chopped hazelnuts to
   decorate

1½ tbsp matzo meal
   or white breadcrumbs

1 tbsp Frangelico or
   other hazelnut liqueur
   (optional)

Chocolate Ganache:

200g double cream

200g good-quality dark
   chocolate (min. 60%
   cocoa solids), chopped

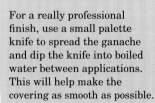

For a really professional finish, use a small palette knife to spread the ganache and dip the knife into boiled water between applications. This will help make the covering as smooth as possible.

* Preheat the oven to 190°C/fan 170°C/gas mark 5. Grease and line a 25cm round, springform cake tin.

* Melt the chocolate in a bowl set over a pan of gently simmering water, making sure the water does not touch the base of the bowl. Remove from the heat and set aside.

* Beat the butter and sugar using a wooden spoon or electric mixer until light and fluffy. Add the egg yolks one at a time, beating well after each addition. Stir in the melted chocolate, then the ground hazelnuts and matzo meal or breadcrumbs. Add the Frangelico, if using.

* In a large bowl, beat the egg whites until stiff. Gently fold them into the chocolate mixture with a large metal spoon.

* Pour the mixture into the tin, spreading it evenly. Bake for about 40–50 minutes or until a skewer inserted into the centre comes out clean. Leave to cool in the tin for a few minutes, then turn out on to a wire rack to cool completely.

* To make the chocolate ganache, place the double cream in a small saucepan and bring just to the boil, then remove from the heat. Add the chocolate, stirring until thoroughly combined. Leave to cool completely.

* Once the ganache is cool and has thickened a little, use it to cover the top and sides of the cake. If you want a more 'frosted' look then beat the ganache with a whisk to your desired consistency. Decorate with chopped hazelnuts and serve with whipped cream or crème fraîche.

Smoked Chilli Chocolate Cake

MARCUS BAWDON

Marcus devised this cake for an event with the theme 'Devilishly Devon'. He added ancho chillies from the South Devon Chilli Farm to give his cake some devilish heat and local provenance. Chilli and chocolate is an established flavour combination and this cake has a smoky, fruity, spicy taste. If you can't get smoked butter, you can use regular unsalted.

SERVES 12

200g good-quality dark
   chocolate (min. 70%
   cocoa solids), broken up
200g butter, diced
50g plain flour
50g ground almonds
75g soft light brown sugar
5 eggs, separated
1 dried ancho chilli
   (smoked chilli), ground
   to a fine powder
100g golden caster sugar
1 red chilli, to decorate
   (optional)

Smoked Chocolate Icing:

100g good-quality dark
   chocolate (min. 70% cocoa
   solids), broken up
50g smoked butter (use
   regular unsalted butter
   if you can't get smoked)

✳ Preheat the oven to 180°C/fan 160°C/gas mark 4. Grease and line a 20cm round, springform cake tin.

✳ Place the chocolate and butter in a bowl set over a pan of gently simmering water, making sure the water does not touch the base of the bowl. Gently stir until melted and combined, then remove from the heat and set aside.

✳ Sift the flour into a bowl and stir through the almonds. In a separate bowl whisk the brown sugar and egg yolks until thick and creamy, then stir in the melted chocolate until combined, and add the chilli.

✳ In a large bowl, whisk the egg whites and the caster sugar until soft peaks form. Gently fold the flour mixture into the chocolate mixture using a large metal spoon, then fold in the egg whites using a large metal spoon, being careful not to knock any air out.

✳ Pour the mixture into the tin and spread evenly. Bake for 40 minutes, until still slightly sticky and fudgy in the middle. Leave to cool completely in the tin before turning out on to a wire rack.

✳ To make the smoked chocolate icing, place the chocolate and butter in a bowl set over a pan of gently simmering water, making sure the water does not touch the base of the bowl. Gently stir until melted and combined, then remove from the heat and leave to cool and thicken slightly.

✳ Once cool, pour it over the top of the cake. Decorate the cake with a chilli, if liked, then enjoy with lashings of clotted cream.

Chocolate Beetroot Cake

WITH CANDIED BEETROOT

LAURA KEY

This cake was originally made for a 'Mad Hatter's Tea Party' themed club event, since some people might consider it mad to use beetroot in a cake! But it's not – chocolate and beetroot go fabulously together. The vegetable adds a lovely, sweet stickiness to the cake, as well as plenty of vibrant colour.

SERVES 16

250g good-quality dark chocolate (min. 60–70% cocoa solids)

3 eggs

250g light muscovado sugar

4 tbsp clear honey

½ tsp vanilla extract

80g plain flour

50g ground almonds

1 tsp baking powder

¼ tsp salt

25g cocoa powder

250g raw beetroot, washed, trimmed, finely chopped

50ml strong black coffee

30ml sunflower oil

1 tbsp Chambord

1 tbsp red food colouring

Candied Beetroot:

100g granulated sugar, plus 2 tbsp for the coating

100g raw beetroot, peeled and grated

Chocolate Icing:

150g good-quality dark chocolate (min. 60–70% cocoa solids), broken up

3 tbsp strong black coffee

1 tsp vanilla extract

3 tbsp clear honey

* Preheat the oven to 170°C/fan 150°C/gas mark 3½. Grease and line a 20cm round, loose-bottomed cake tin.

* Break up the chocolate and melt it in a bowl set over a pan of gently simmering water, making sure the water does not touch the base of the bowl. Remove from the heat and set aside to cool.

* Beat the eggs, sugar, honey and vanilla extract using a wooden spoon or electric mixer until light and fluffy. Fold in the flour, ground almonds, baking powder, salt and cocoa until thoroughly combined. Stir in the melted chocolate, beetroot, coffee, sunflower oil, Chambord and red colouring.

* Pour the mixture into the tin, spreading it evenly. Bake for 1½ hours, then cover the cake with foil and bake for a further 30 minutes (it takes this length of time to cook the beetroot). The cake should be firm and a skewer inserted into the centre should come out with a few crumbs clinging to it. Turn out on to a wire rack to cool.

* To make the candied beetroot slivers, place the sugar and 100ml water in a saucepan and bring to the boil, stirring to dissolve the sugar. Add the beetroot and cook until the beetroot softens (about 10–15 minutes, depending on the size of the pieces), then drain and leave to cool slightly before coating in the extra sugar. Set aside.

* To make the icing, place the chocolate, coffee, vanilla extract and honey in a bowl set over a pan of gently simmering water, stirring to melt and combine. Remove from the heat and leave to cool and thicken.

* Once cool, spoon the icing over the top of the cake, easing it down the sides to cover the whole cake. Arrange the candied beetroot on top to decorate.

Coconut Paradise Cake

SERRIKA JOSEPH

If you're a fan of coconut, you'll fall head over heels for this flavoursome sponge, filled with coconut buttercream and finished with an indulgent coating of rich, creamy milk chocolate ganache. Decorate with pieces of Bounty bar or generous shavings of toasted fresh coconut. Ideally you should make this cake the day before you want to serve it to allow the ganache enough time to set completely.

SERVES 10

225g soft margarine
(such as Stork)
225g golden caster sugar
3 eggs
225g self-raising flour
150ml milk
1½ tsp baking powder
100g creamed coconut, grated
1 Bounty bar, cut into 8,
to decorate

Coconut Buttercream Filling:

75g soft margarine
175g icing sugar, sifted
1 tbsp vanilla extract
or coconut rum (such
as Malibu)
25g desiccated coconut

Chocolate Ganache Topping:

150ml double cream
150g good-quality milk
chocolate (min. 34% cocoa
solids), finely chopped

* Preheat the oven to 190°C/fan 170°C/gas mark 5. Grease and line two 20cm round sandwich tins.

* Beat the margarine and sugar using a wooden spoon or electric mixer until light and fluffy. Add the eggs one at a time, beating well after each addition, and adding a tablespoon of the flour with the final egg to help prevent curdling, then add the milk. Gradually fold in the remaining flour and baking powder, until thoroughly combined, then fold in the creamed coconut.

* Divide the mixture between the tins, spreading it evenly. Bake for about 25 minutes, until golden and the tops spring back when gently pressed. Leave to cool in the tins for 5 minutes, then turn out on to wire racks to cool completely.

* For the buttercream filling, beat the margarine until very soft and creamy. Gradually beat in the icing sugar, then the vanilla extract or coconut rum. Stir in the desiccated coconut. Add more icing sugar or liquid according to your preferred consistency, then spread the filling over one cake and place the other on top to sandwich them together.

* To make the chocolate ganache, heat the cream in a small pan over a low to medium heat. Place the chocolate in a mixing bowl, and once the cream is just boiling pour it over the chocolate and stir until melted and smooth. Allow to cool slightly, until thickened, then use to cover the top and sides of the whole cake.

* Decorate the cake with the Bounty bar pieces and allow the ganache to set completely, ideally overnight, before serving.

Dark Chocolate Marmalade Cake

CATRIONA ROSCOE

Inspired by one of her favourite treats – Jaffa cakes – Catriona created this dark and decadent sponge with delicious lumps of marmalade. If not using a Terry's Chocolate Orange, make sure to use a good-quality, dark, orange-flavoured chocolate, but when it comes to the marmalade, the cheaper or economy brands are just as successful as the high-end alternatives.

SERVES 8–10

250g butter
200g dark orange chocolate
  (such as Terry's Dark
  Chocolate Orange or
  Lindt Orange Intense),
  broken up
6 tbsp fine-cut marmalade
250g caster sugar
4 large eggs
250g self-raising flour
2 tbsp cocoa powder
Terry's Chocolate Orange
  segments, or other
  chocolates, to decorate

Chocolate Buttercream:

100g good-quality dark
  chocolate (min. 60–70%
  cocoa solids), broken up
200g butter, softened
400g icing sugar
2 tbsp cocoa powder

* Preheat the oven to 175°C/fan 155°C/gas mark 4. Grease and line two 20cm round, springform cake tins.

* Place the butter in a saucepan, and just before it has completely melted add 100g of the orange chocolate. Remove the pan from the heat and continue stirring with a wooden spoon until the butter and chocolate are fully melted and combined.

* Stir in the marmalade and mix well to break down any big lumps (small lumps are fine and taste delicious in the finished cake). Add the sugar and eggs and stir until thoroughly combined.

* Sift in the flour and cocoa powder and gently fold in until just combined, then fold in the remaining orange chocolate (this is quite a runny batter). Pour the mixture into the tins, spreading it evenly.

* Bake for approximately 35 minutes or until a skewer inserted into the centre comes out clean. Leave to cool in the tins for 10 minutes before turning out on to a wire rack to cool completely.

* Meanwhile, make the chocolate buttercream. Melt the chocolate in a bowl set over a pan of gently simmering water, making sure the water does not touch the base of the bowl. Remove from the heat and set aside to cool.

* Beat the butter for a few minutes to soften and loosen it, then sift in the icing sugar and cocoa. Keep beating until you have a light, fluffy buttercream. Beat in the cooled but still-molten chocolate until combined. Once the cakes are cool, sandwich together with a layer of the buttercream, then cover the top with a thin layer of the remainder. Decorate with chocolate orange segments or your choice of chocolate decorations.

Buttermilk Chocolate Cake
WITH WHITE CHOCOLATE & MASCARPONE FILLING

SARAH MILLIGAN

This cake made its national TV debut on a special CCC feature on The One Show. *Sarah decorated her original cake with* The One Show *logo printed on sugarpaste icing. You can customise yours in a similar way for a birthday or special occasion (printed icing sheets can be ordered from online suppliers), but for a simpler, more everyday treat, simply dust with icing sugar.*

SERVES 20

300g plain flour
1 tsp bicarbonate of soda
1 tsp salt
120g butter, softened
300g caster sugar
2 large eggs
1 tsp vanilla paste
30g cocoa powder, mixed with
    5–6 tbsp warm water
240ml buttermilk
1 tbsp white wine vinegar

White Chocolate Filling:
300g white chocolate
300g mascarpone cheese

Topping (optional):
4 tbsp apricot jam
food colouring paste (colour
    of choice)
500g ready-to-roll white
    sugarpaste
icing sugar, to roll out
1 x printed icing sheet of your
    choice (optional)

* Preheat the oven to 190°C/fan 170°C/gas mark 5. Grease and line a 24cm square cake tin.

* Sift together the flour, bicarbonate of soda and salt and set aside. Beat the butter and sugar using a wooden spoon or electric mixer until pale. Add the eggs one at a time, beating well after each addition, and adding a tablespoon of the flour with the final egg to help prevent curdling.

* Add the vanilla paste and cocoa powder paste to the bowl and mix thoroughly until evenly combined. Slowly pour in half the buttermilk, beat until well mixed, then mix in half the flour. Repeat with the remaining buttermilk and flour, then add the vinegar. Beat until thoroughly combined.

* Pour the mixture into the tin and cook for about 50 minutes or until the top of the cake is springy to the touch and a skewer inserted into the centre comes out clean. Leave to cool completely in the tin.

* When the cake is completely cold turn it upside down and cut it in half horizontally (it is easier to do this the day after it's baked as the cake is firmer).

* Make the filling. Melt the white chocolate in a heatproof bowl set over a pan of simmering water, making sure the water does not touch the base of the bowl. When it is melted and smooth, remove from the heat and leave to cool a little. Mix in the mascarpone, until it is thoroughly combined, then set aside to cool completely. When cool, use the filling to sandwich the cake layers together.

* If you are making the topping, cover the cake with cling film and chill for an hour or so to firm up.

* Warm and sieve the apricot jam and use a pastry brush to brush all over the cake.

* Mix the food colouring paste of your choice into the sugarpaste and knead until evenly coloured. Dust a surface with icing sugar and roll out two-thirds of the sugarpaste, turning it frequently and using lots of icing sugar to roll it out until it is around 3–4mm thick and wide enough to cover the whole cake.

* Pick up the sugarpaste over a rolling pin and carefully drape it over the cake. Press it gently down the sides of the cake, smoothing out any bumps, then cut off any excess. Using a small pastry brush, carefully brush off any excess icing sugar. Stick on the printed icing sheet using the jam.

Chocolate Honeycomb Truffle Cake

GARY MORTON

This magnificent cake is a feast both for the eyes and for the appetite, with its homemade honeycomb, truffles and ganache. If you like, you can customise the truffles with your favourite liqueur. Just try not to gobble them all up before you get round to decorating the cake!

SERVES 15–20

450g self-raising flour
6 tbsp cocoa powder
450g butter, very soft
450g caster sugar
8 eggs

Truffles:

100g good-quality dark
 chocolate (min. 60–70%
 cocoa solids), finely chopped
100ml double cream
2–3 tsp of your favourite
 liqueur, to taste
cocoa powder, to dust

Honeycomb:

80g butter
160g caster sugar
80g golden syrup
2 tsp bicarbonate of soda

Frosting:

250ml double cream
300g good-quality dark
 chocolate (min. 60–70%
 cocoa solids), broken up
20g butter, diced

TIP

Divide the truffle mixture in half before adding the liqueur and you can use two different flavours. Spiced rum and whisky both work nicely!

* Start by making the mixture for the truffles. Place the chopped dark chocolate in a bowl. Heat the cream in a small saucepan until it is almost at boiling point, then remove from the heat and pour it over the chocolate. Stir gently until the chocolate has melted, then stir in your chosen liqueur. Pour the mixture into a small, shallow dish and leave to cool, then place in the fridge until firm.

* Make the honeycomb. Line a baking tray with non-stick baking paper. Place all the ingredients except the bicarbonate of soda in a pan over a low heat to melt, then very slowly bring to the boil. Boil gently until the mixture turns a deep golden honeycomb colour. If it starts to colour quicker on one side then give the mixture a swirl, don't stir.

* Once a golden colour has been achieved (after about 5 minutes), remove the pan from the heat and add the bicarbonate of soda and stir in gently – it will cause the mixture to expand. Pour into the tray and leave to cool and set. Break into chunks and store in an airtight container until needed.

* Preheat the oven to 180°C/fan 160°C/gas mark 4. Grease and line two 20cm round, springform cake tins.

* To make the sponges, place the measured flour in a bowl, then remove six tablespoonfuls and return them to the bag. Replace with the cocoa powder. Add the remaining cake ingredients to the bowl and whisk until thoroughly combined. Divide the mixture between the tins, spreading it evenly. Bake for about 1 hour or until a skewer inserted into the centre comes out clean. Turn out on to a wire rack to cool completely.

CONTINUED ▶

* To make the frosting, bring the cream just to boiling point, then remove from the heat and set aside. Melt the chocolate in a bowl set over a pan of gently simmering water, making sure the water does not touch the base of the bowl. Remove from the heat and gradually stir in the warm cream, until smooth and glossy. Stir in the butter.

* To assemble the cake, make sure the sponges are level when they are on top of each other, if not slice off the offending area. Grind half the honeycomb, either in a food processor or by beating it with a rolling pin, then place 4–5 tablespoons of the chocolate frosting in a small bowl and mix in enough ground honeycomb to give a fairly thick mixture – this will be the filling.

* Sandwich the two sponges together with the filling, then use the remaining frosting to cover the top and sides of the whole cake, using a palette knife to spread and smooth it.

* Finally, finish the truffles. Dust your hands with cocoa powder, then take teaspoon-sized amounts of the truffle mixture and roll into small balls, until all the mixture has been used. Dust the balls with cocoa powder. Decorate the top of the cake with the truffles, shards of honeycomb and some of the remaining ground honeycomb.

Chocolate Orange Disaster Cake

RACHEL BAXTER

This cake is so-called because it almost didn't see the light of day, when Rach sadly dropped it on her way to the first-ever Clandestine Cake Club meeting! However, it has since been made successfully and enjoyed by many club members. Hopefully your attempt at her recipe won't end up on the floor…! See photo overleaf.

SERVES 8

100g butter, softened
100g caster sugar
3 eggs
100g self-raising flour
25g cocoa powder
1 tsp baking powder
grated zest of 1 orange
1–2 tsp milk

Icing:

75g good-quality dark
  chocolate (min. 70%
  cocoa solids)
100g butter, softened
200g icing sugar
generous dash of Grand
  Marnier

Decoration:

1 orange, peeled and
  segmented
1 tbsp Grand Marnier
OR candied orange zest
  (see Tip)

TIP
To make candied orange zest, peel long, thin strips with a zester. Gently heat 75g sugar and 75ml water in a small pan, stir to dissolve, then increase the heat and simmer for 2–3 minutes to make a light syrup. Add the strands of zest and cook for 2–3 minutes. Remove and place on baking paper to cool.

✳ Preheat the oven to 175°C/fan 155°C/gas mark 4. Grease and line two 18cm round sandwich tins.

✳ Beat the butter and sugar using a wooden spoon or electric mixer until light and fluffy. Add the eggs one at a time, beating well after each addition, and adding a tablespoon of the flour with the final egg to help prevent curdling. Sift in the remaining flour, cocoa powder, baking powder and gently fold in together with the orange zest. Add a splash of milk if the batter is too thick – it needs to have a dropping consistency.

✳ Divide the mixture between the tins, spreading it evenly. Bake for 20 minutes or until a skewer inserted into the centre comes out clean. Leave to cool in the tins for 10 minutes then turn out on to a wire rack to cool completely.

✳ To make the icing, melt the chocolate in a bowl set over a pan of gently simmering water, making sure the water does not touch the base of the bowl, then remove from the heat. Beat the butter and icing sugar together until light and fluffy, then mix in the Grand Marnier and the chocolate.

✳ To assemble, spread the icing generously over the top of one cake, cover with the second cake, then spread the remaining icing on top.

✳ To decorate with soaked orange segments, put the segments in a bowl, pour over the Grand Marnier and leave for about half an hour, then arrange on the cake. Alternatively, this cake looks lovely decorated with candied orange zest (see Tip).

CHOCOLATE
ORANGE
DISASTER
CAKE

CHOCOLATE & MARMITE CARAMEL CAKE

Chocolate & Marmite Caramel Cake

BECS RIVETT

Marmite: you either love it or hate it, but this recipe will see many sceptics changing their minds. The saltiness of the Marmite in the buttercream adds extra depth and helps bring out the taste of the caramel (in a similar way to salted caramel). People who tried this cake at a club event without knowing the 'secret' ingredient said it tasted like coffee. They were surprised and delighted by the truth! See photo on previous page.

SERVES 8–10

175g dark chocolate (min. 70% cocoa solids), broken up
175g butter, softened
175g caster sugar
4 large eggs, separated
90g ground almonds
90g plain flour, sifted

Caramel Marmite Buttercream:

120g butter, at room temperature
440g soft light brown sugar
180ml milk
2 tsp Marmite, or more to taste
480g icing sugar, sifted

* Preheat the oven to 180°C/fan 160°C/gas mark 4. Grease and line two 18cm round sandwich tins.

* Melt the chocolate in a bowl set over a pan of gently simmering water, making sure the water does not touch the base of the bowl. Stir gently, then remove from the heat.

* Beat the butter and sugar with a wooden spoon or electric mixer until light and fluffy. Add the egg yolks one at a time, beating well after each addition, then add the melted chocolate and ground almonds.

* In a separate bowl, whisk the egg whites to soft peaks. Use a large metal spoon to gently fold the whisked egg whites and sifted flour into the mixture bit by bit until completely incorporated. Divide the mixture between the tins and spread evenly. Bake for 18–20 minutes, until springy to the touch. Leave to cool for a couple of minutes in the tins before turning out on to a wire rack to cool completely.

* Make the buttercream. In a large saucepan, melt the butter over a low heat, then mix in the brown sugar, milk and Marmite, stirring until it comes to the boil. Boil for 1 minute, then remove from the heat and transfer to a large bowl. Taste and add more Marmite if desired (remember that it will be diluted by the icing sugar).

* Whisk in half the icing sugar and then leave to cool, checking and stirring regularly to regulate the consistency. Once cool, whisk in the remaining icing sugar. If it is still runny, sift in enough icing sugar to reach a spreadable consistency.

* To assemble, spread a third of the buttercream over one of the cooled cakes, then sandwich with the other cake. Cover the top and sides of the whole cake with the remaining buttercream, smoothing it with a palette knife.

Chocolate Nut Rum Cake

LYNN HILL

This velvety dark chocolate cake consists of a rum-soaked sponge, a rich chocolate ganache and chopped nuts inside and out. It is a challenge to self-control, and definitely one that has 'eat me' written all over it. See photo overleaf.

SERVES 12

120g good-quality dark chocolate (min. 70% cocoa solids), broken up

250g butter, softened

250g soft light brown sugar

1 tsp vanilla extract, or the scraped seeds of 1 vanilla pod

4 large eggs

250g self-raising flour, sifted

80g mixed nuts, chopped, to fill and decorate

Chocolate Rum Ganache:

250g good-quality milk chocolate (min. 34% cocoa solids), chopped

100g good-quality dark chocolate (min. 70% cocoa solids), chopped

250ml double cream

2 tbsp dark rum

Rum Syrup:

60g granulated sugar

3 tbsp dark rum

✳ Start by making the ganache, ideally a day before needed, as the optimum spreadable consistency is achieved after 24 hours at room temperature. Place all the chocolate in a bowl. Heat the cream in a small pan until bubbles form around the edge, then pour it over the chocolate and stir gently until smooth. Stir in the rum.

✳ Transfer to a bowl and leave to cool, then cover and leave to stand overnight or for a minimum of 6 hours. This can be hastened by placing the mixture in the fridge, but stir it occasionally to prevent the edges solidifying and bring back to room temperature before decorating your cake. This can be achieved by giving the whole ganache a good mix using a wooden spoon or spatula.

✳ To make the cake, preheat the oven to 190°C/fan 170°C/gas mark 5. Grease and line two 20cm round sandwich tins.

✳ Melt the chocolate in a bowl set over a pan of gently simmering water, making sure the water does not touch the base of the bowl. Stir gently, then remove from the heat and set aside to cool but not set.

✳ Beat the butter and sugar using a wooden spoon or electric mixer until light and fluffy. Add the vanilla and mix until combined. Add the eggs one at a time, beating well after each addition, and adding a tablespoon of the flour with the final egg to help prevent curdling. Beat in the cooled, melted chocolate and mix until thoroughly combined, then sift in the remaining flour and mix well.

✳ Divide the mixture between the tins, spreading it evenly. Bake in the oven for 20–25 minutes or until a skewer inserted into the centre comes out clean. Leave to cool in the tins for 10 minutes before turning out on to a wire rack to cool completely.

CONTINUED

Chocolate Nut Rum Cake
CONTINUED

* To make the syrup, gently heat 125ml water with the sugar in a small pan, stirring to dissolve the sugar. Increase the heat and simmer for 3–4 minutes, then remove from the heat and stir in the rum. Leave to cool.

* To assemble the cake, cut both cakes in half horizontally with a serrated knife. Place one layer on a plate and brush generously with syrup. Spread over a thin layer of ganache, right to the edge. Scatter with chopped nuts, then cover with another cake layer. Repeat for each layer, but leaving the top layer uncovered.

* Use a small palette knife dipped in boiling water then dried to spread any ganache that is still firm. Cover the top of the cake with the remaining ganache and decorate with the remaining chopped nuts.

White Chocolate & Raspberry Loaf

AMANDA WOODWARD

Raspberries and white chocolate are a match made in heaven, especially in cakes. This is a very easy recipe, though do take care not to crush the berries when folding them into the batter, so that the juice doesn't ooze out. Decorate with fresh raspberries for extra spring-like prettiness.

SERVES 8–10

125g butter, softened

175g caster sugar

2 large eggs

175g self-raising flour

4 tbsp milk

150g raspberries, plus
  a few extra to decorate

125g white cooking chocolate

∗ Preheat the oven to 180°C/fan 160°C/gas mark 4. Grease and line a 900g loaf tin.

∗ Beat the butter and sugar using a wooden spoon or electric mixer until light and fluffy. Add the eggs one at a time, beating well after each addition, and adding a tablespoon of the flour with the final egg to help prevent curdling.

∗ Sift in the remaining flour and gently fold in until thoroughly combined. Stir in the milk, then carefully fold in the raspberries, taking care not to squash them.

∗ Spoon the mixture into the tin and spread it out evenly. Bake for 35–40 minutes, or until risen and golden and a skewer inserted into the centre comes out clean. Leave to cool in the tin.

∗ Meanwhile, melt the white chocolate in a heatproof bowl set over a pan of simmering water, making sure the water does not touch the base of the bowl. Remove from the heat and drizzle the chocolate across the top of the cake, then decorate the top with raspberries. Leave the topping to cool and set before tucking in.

Honey Chocolate Cheesecake

DENA HABASHI-AYUB

This is a delicious, no-bake cheesecake, covered in gorgeous honey-flavoured ganache with a show-stopping spiderweb effect. It's not difficult to create but does need a steady hand, so take your time to get the lines perfect.

SERVES 20

450g good-quality dark chocolate (min. 70% cocoa solids)

150g digestive biscuits

50g shortbread biscuits

90g butter, melted

2 tbsp clear honey

360ml double cream

2 tbsp cocoa powder, mixed with enough hot water to make a runny paste

600g full-fat cream cheese

315g caster sugar

Glaze & Decoration:

250ml good-quality dark chocolate (min. 70% cocoa solids), finely chopped

250ml double cream

2 tbsp clear honey

100g white chocolate

TIP

Ganache sets quite quickly so ensure that the white chocolate is warmed in advance, ready for piping your decoration.

* Line a 25cm round, springform cake tin with cling film. Melt the chocolate in a bowl set over a pan of gently simmering water, making sure the water does not touch the base of the bowl. Stir gently, then remove from the heat and set aside to cool (but not set).

* Put both types of biscuits in a blender and blitz to coarse crumbs (the coarser, the better). Add the melted butter and honey and blend until evenly mixed. Pour the crumbs into the cake tin and press down using the back of a large metal spoon to get a nice smooth surface. Cover the tin with cling film and leave in the freezer for at least 1 hour.

* Whip the cream to soft peaks. Add the cooled, melted chocolate and cocoa paste to the cream and mix well. In a separate bowl, beat the cream cheese and sugar until combined. Carefully fold in the cream and chocolate mixture using a large metal spoon. Spoon on to the biscuit base, smooth the top and cover with cling film. Freeze for at least 1 hour.

* For the glaze, place the dark chocolate in a bowl. Heat the cream and honey in a small pan until bubbles form at the edge, then pour over the chocolate and stir gently until smooth. Leave to cool slightly.

* Melt the white chocolate in a bowl set over a pan of gently simmering water, making sure the water does not touch the base of the bowl. It needs to be melted to piping consistency (not too thick or runny), then transfer to a piping bag fitted with a small, plain nozzle.

* Place the cheesecake on a wire rack set over a baking tray and pour the ganache on to the centre of the cake. Using a palette knife, spread it outwards from the centre so it covers the entire cake.

* Pipe the white chocolate on top, starting in the centre and piping an even spiral outwards. Using the tip of a sharp knife or a cocktail stick, drag straight lines through the spiral, starting alternately from the centre (dragging outwards) and the edges (dragging inwards). You will be left with a beautiful, two-tone, chocolate spiderweb.

Chocolate & Maple Brunch Cake

CHARLIE SCOTT-KING

With coffee, yoghurt, bran and maple syrup, this cake combines some of our favourite breakfast ingredients and turns them into a mid-morning treat! The yoghurt in this recipe makes this cake moist and rich.

SERVES 16

200ml strong hot black coffee

100g good-quality dark chocolate (min. 50–60% cocoa solids), chopped

200g plain flour

2 tsp baking powder

100g cocoa powder

3 large eggs

250g demerara sugar

100g natural yoghurt

100ml vegetable oil

50g porridge oats or bran

pinch of salt

Maple Topping:

200g icing sugar

1 tbsp maple syrup

✳ Preheat the oven to 190°C/fan 170°C/gas mark 5. Grease and line a 23cm square cake tin.

✳ Pour the hot coffee over the chocolate and leave for 10 minutes. Sift the flour, baking powder and cocoa into a bowl and set aside.

✳ In a separate bowl beat the eggs and sugar until combined. Give the chocolate mixture a stir, making sure it is free of lumps (if there are still lumps, warm it in the microwave or in a pan set over a low heat for 1 minute), then pour over the sugar and egg mixture and stir to combine. Add the yoghurt and oil, beating well to combine, then gently fold in the flour mixture, oats or bran and salt until thoroughly combined.

✳ Pour the mixture into the tin, spreading it evenly. Bake for about 35 minutes or until a skewer inserted into the centre comes out clean. Leave to cool in the tin for 5 minutes then turn out on to a wire rack to cool completely.

✳ For the topping, mix the icing sugar and maple syrup in a bowl, then slowly add 1–2 tablespoons of cold water until you have a thick white icing. Pour this over the top of the cake.

Dark Chocolate & Amaretto Cake

CARMELA HAYES

This cake packs quite an almondy punch, with both amaretti biscuits and amaretto liqueur. It is best made by hand, rather than with a mixer, to help retain some texture in the biscuits and chocolate. Pane degli angeli (an Italian vanilla-flavoured raising agent) can be purchased from Italian delis; however, one teaspoon of baking powder and two teaspoons of vanilla extract is fine as a substitute.

SERVES 10–12

4 large eggs

50g caster sugar

200g self-raising flour

100g ground almonds

1 sachet of pane degli angeli or 1 tsp baking powder mixed with 2 tsp vanilla extract

200g butter, melted

200g good-quality dark chocolate (min. 60–70% cocoa solids), chopped

200g amaretti biscuits (the hard ones), crushed

2 tbsp amaretto liqueur

* Preheat the oven to 200°C/fan 180°C/gas mark 6. Grease and line a 23cm round, loose-bottomed cake tin.

* In a large mixing bowl beat the eggs and sugar using a wooden spoon. Add the flour, ground almonds, pane degli angeli and melted butter and mix well, then stir in the chocolate, amaretti biscuits and amaretto liqueur, mixing well.

* Pour the mixture into the tin, spreading it evenly. Bake the cake for 45–50 minutes until the top is firm to the touch and a skewer inserted into the centre comes out clean.

* Leave the cake to cool in the tin for about 10 minutes, then remove from the tin and place on a wire rack to cool completely.

Courgette Cocoa Cake

LYNN HILL

I love courgette in cakes – it adds moisture and texture yet still allows the other flavours to shine through. Finished with a simple cream cheese frosting and chopped hazelnuts, this cake is extremely moreish. If you can get them, courgette flowers make a lovely decoration for special occasions.

SERVES 10–12

325g courgettes
  (about 2 medium
  courgettes), peeled
300g self-raising flour
½ tsp baking powder
3 eggs, beaten
375g golden caster sugar
175ml rapeseed oil
  or sunflower oil
50g cocoa powder
100g hazelnuts, chopped,
  to decorate
courgette flowers, to
  decorate (optional)

Cream Cheese Frosting:

170g butter, softened
255g full-fat cream cheese,
  from the fridge
85g icing sugar

For a coffee-flavoured version of this cake, replace the cocoa powder in the batter with 1 tbsp of instant espresso powder and add ½ tsp of espresso powder to the frosting.

* Preheat the oven to 190°C/fan 170°C/gas mark 5. Grease and line a 20cm round, springform cake tin.

* Grate the courgettes into a sieve and leave to drain while you make the cake. Combine the flour and baking powder and set aside. Beat the eggs and sugar using a wooden spoon or electric mixer until light and fluffy. Still beating, add the oil then the cocoa powder. Beat together for a couple of minutes.

* Squeeze the grated courgettes in kitchen paper to remove any excess liquid, then add them to the flour mixture, stirring to ensure all the courgette is coated in flour and that there are no lumps. Add the courgette mixture to the egg mixture and gently fold in until thoroughly combined.

* Transfer the mixture to the tin and spread evenly. Bake for 1¼ hours or until a skewer inserted into the centre comes out clean. Leave to cool in the tin for a few minutes before turning out on to a wire rack to cool completely.

* Make the frosting. Beat the butter until smooth. Add the cream cheese and mix until combined, then sift in the icing sugar and beat until light and fluffy.

* To assemble, cut the cake in half horizontally and spread a thin layer of the frosting over the bottom layer, then sandwich the two layers together. Cover the sides and top of the cake with the remaining frosting. Decorate the sides of the cake with the hazelnuts and the top with courgette flowers, if using.

There are so many great excuses for cake throughout the year: not least birthdays, Valentine's, Mother's Day, Halloween, Christmas and New Year. Each month brings delicious opportunities to serve up a slice of something sweet. These events and holidays always give club members a chance to get wildly artistic and have some fun, and some of our most creative cakes are baked at these times of year. This chapter is packed full of some of the very best of our club members' seasonal cakey creations. You may even want to bake one for your wedding cake!

Celebration
Cakes

Valentine's Achy Cakey Heart Cake

RACHEL MCGRATH

With its pink sponge, red glaze and liberal scattering of edible sprinkles (or glitter!), this cake is a sure-fire way of convincing someone to be your Valentine, especially when baked in a heart-shaped bundt tin. This cake will keep for about three days if stored in an airtight container.

SERVES 12

225g butter, softened
450g golden caster sugar
4 eggs
350g plain flour
½ tsp bicarbonate of soda
½ tsp salt
250ml thick vanilla yoghurt
1 tsp vanilla extract
pink food colouring paste

Glaze:

200g icing sugar
warm water, to mix
red food colouring paste

TIP

You can bake this cake in a 23cm round, springform cake tin. Take care not to fill it more than three-quarters full, and be prepared that the baking time may be slightly shorter; keep a close eye on it and start testing with a skewer at 50 minutes to check whether the sponge is baked through.

✳ Preheat the oven to 170°C/fan 150°C/gas mark 3½. Grease and flour a heart-shaped bundt tin, about 2–2.5 litres in capacity (or see Tip if you want to use a round tin).

✳ Beat the butter and sugar using a wooden spoon or electric mixer until light and fluffy. Add the eggs one at a time, beating well after each addition, and adding a tablespoon of the flour with the final egg to help prevent curdling.

✳ Mix the flour, bicarbonate of soda and salt in a bowl. In a separate bowl, combine the yoghurt, vanilla and a small, pea-sized amount of pink food colouring. Adding this to the liquid ingredients will prevent the flour being overworked later.

✳ Sift a third of the flour mix into the egg mixture and mix until just combined, then add half the yoghurt mixture. Repeat until everything is thoroughly combined. Don't worry too much if the mixture isn't all one shade of pink; it's quite pretty to have a ripple effect. Spoon the mixture into the tin, smoothing the top. This mixture doesn't rise much, so fill the tin about three-quarters full.

✳ Bake for 1 hour or until a skewer inserted into the centre comes out clean. Leave to cool completely in the tin, then turn out on to a large plate or board.

✳ To make the glaze, add about two tablespoons of warm water to the icing sugar – it should be thin enough to run with ease when you tilt the bowl. Add enough food colouring to make the glaze your desired shade of red, then drizzle over the cake. If you wish to decorate it, scatter over any sprinkles or decorations while the glaze is still wet.

Finnish Lemon Mother's Day Cake

RIIKKA HARIKKALA

This pretty cake is served in Finland at many types of celebrations, most notably for Mother's Day, which is celebrated there in May. But with its lemony freshness and rich mascarpone filling, it is equally delicious at any time of the year. Replace the potato flour with cocoa powder for a chocolate variation.

SERVES 15–20

5 eggs
200g caster sugar
150g plain flour
4 tbsp potato flour
1 tsp baking powder
ready-made sugarpaste
   flowers, to decorate
   (optional)

Lemon Syrup:
juice of 2 lemons
150g icing sugar

Fillings:
200ml double cream
200g mascarpone
2 tbsp icing sugar
325g lemon curd, plus extra
   to decorate (optional)

Icing:
600ml double cream
1 tbsp vanilla caster sugar
   (see Tip on page 116) or
   1 tbsp custard powder
   (optional)

* Preheat the oven to 180°C/fan 160°C/gas mark 4. Grease and line the base and sides of a 23cm round cake tin. Try to leave some extra baking paper above the sides of the tin – this will help the cake rise and colour evenly.

* Whisk the eggs with the sugar until pale, light and doubled in volume and the whisk leaves a ribbon trail when lifted out.

* In a separate bowl, combine the flours and baking powder, then sift the dry ingredients over the egg mixture in two batches. Fold in gently until thoroughly combined.

* Pour the mixture into the tin, spreading it evenly. Bake the cake for 35–45 minutes, until risen and golden and a skewer inserted into the centre comes out clean. Leave in the tin for a few minutes, before turning out on to a wire rack to cool completely.

* Meanwhile, make the syrup. Put the lemon juice and icing sugar in a small saucepan and heat, stirring gently, until the sugar has completely dissolved. Remove from the heat and set aside to cool.

* Cut the cooled cake into three equal layers. Trim the top, if necessary, to even it out. Douse the top of each layer with the lemon syrup. Don't oversoak or your cake may become soggy.

* To make the filling, whip the cream until just beginning to thicken, add the mascarpone and icing sugar and whisk until thick and smooth.

* To assemble, place the top layer of your cake upside down on a serving plate and spread half the mascarpone cream over the top. Gently spread half the lemon curd over the mascarpone. Cover with the middle layer of cake and repeat with the remaining filling and lemon curd, then place the bottom layer of the cake on top, so that the even base becomes the top of the cake. If you are preparing this cake

CONTINUED ➤

in advance of your occasion you can now put the cake into the fridge overnight and ice it just before serving.

✳ For the icing, whip the cream to piping consistency. You can add vanilla sugar for flavour, if you like, or custard powder to help the cream withstand the heat during summer months. Spread a thin layer of the cream on top of the cake and pipe the rest on to the sides using a piping bag fitted with a star nozzle.

✳ Put some lemon curd in a squeezy bottle or piping bag fitted with a small plain nozzle and use to decorate the top of the cake. Decorate with sugarpaste flowers, if you wish.

St Paddy's Day Guinness Loaf

LYNN HILL

Moist, moreish and with a texture a bit like malt loaf, this cake is loaded with fruit that has been soaked overnight in your favourite stout. Remember to reserve the remaining Guinness for the batter. This will keep for up to a week wrapped in greaseproof paper in an airtight container.

SERVES 12

350g mixed dried fruit
1 x 330ml bottle of Guinness
2 eggs, beaten
100g soft light brown sugar
100g dark muscovado sugar
270g self-raising flour
½ tsp mixed spice

TIP

You can replace the Guinness with 350ml freshly brewed leaf tea, such as Earl Grey. Remember to strain the leaves before pouring over the dried fruit.

✳ Place the dried fruit and Guinness in a bowl, cover and leave overnight to allow the fruit to absorb all the goodness and flavours of the Guinness.

✳ Preheat the oven to 180°C/fan 160°C/gas mark 4. Grease and line a 900g loaf tin.

✳ Stir the beaten eggs into the fruit mixture, then add the sugars, flour and spice, and mix well. Dark sugar can retain large lumps, which are not good when baked, so be sure to mix thoroughly.

✳ Pour the mixture into the tin and spread evenly. Bake for 1–1¼ hours, until a skewer inserted into the centre comes out clean. Leave in the tin to cool completely.

Raspberry Yoghurt Birthday Bundt

RACHEL MCGRATH

This wonderfully light sponge with its pretty pink frosting is brilliant as a girly birthday cake. For something a bit more subtle, it can be frosted in a lighter colour or simply dusted with icing sugar. You can easily adapt the flavour of the sponge by substituting your favourite flavour of yoghurt.

SERVES 12

225g butter, softened
450g golden caster sugar
4 eggs
350g plain flour
½ tsp bicarbonate of soda
½ tsp salt
250ml good-quality thick
   raspberry yoghurt
1 tsp vanilla extract
200g raspberries (optional)
white chocolate or sugar stars,
   to decorate (optional)

Pink Frosting:
200g butter, softened
400g icing sugar
3 tbsp milk
pink food colouring
½ tsp raspberry flavouring
   (optional)

* Preheat the oven to 170°C/fan 150°C/gas mark 3½. Grease and flour a 2.5–3-litre bundt tin.

* Beat the butter and sugar using a wooden spoon or electric mixer until light and fluffy. Add the eggs one at a time, beating well after each addition, and adding a tablespoon of the flour with the final egg to help prevent curdling.

* Mix the remaining flour, bicarbonate of soda and salt in a bowl. In a separate bowl, combine the yoghurt and vanilla.

* Sift a third of the flour mixture into the egg mixture and stir until just combined, then add half the yoghurt mixture. Repeat until everything is thoroughly combined. Mix on a low speed for about 15 seconds or beat with a wooden spoon to give it a good mix. Fold in the raspberries, if using.

* Transfer the mixture to the tin, spreading it evenly. Bake for 1 hour or until a skewer inserted into the centre comes out clean. Leave to cool in the tin.

* To make the frosting, beat the butter until creamy, then slowly add the icing sugar and milk. Add enough food colouring to make the frosting your desired shade of pink, then add the raspberry flavouring, if using. Spread the frosting over the whole cake, then decorate with white chocolate stars, as liked.

Easter Spring Roll

WITH LEMON & HONEY SYLLABUB

CARLA GARDINER

This cake is a gorgeous meringue roulade filled with a tangy lemon and honey syllabub and fresh berries, and has a wonderful light freshness to it, perfect for an Easter treat. Use the baking paper to help you roll it up, but don't panic if the cake cracks – it will still taste gorgeous and you can hide any imperfections with a dusting of icing sugar and some mini chocolate eggs.

SERVES 8

4 egg whites
225g caster sugar
25–35g ground almonds
100g raspberries
100g blueberries
icing sugar, to dust

Lemon & Honey Syllabub:
grated zest and juice of
  1 lemon
4 tbsp clear honey
300ml double cream,
  from the fridge

* Preheat the oven to 220°C/fan 200°C/gas mark 7. Line a 32 x 23cm Swiss roll tin.

* In a scrupulously clean bowl whisk the egg whites until stiff. Add the sugar a little at a time, beating continuously. Continue to beat until thick and glossy.

* Spread the mixture over the baking sheet, then generously cover with the ground almonds. Bake in the oven for about 10 minutes or until golden brown and the top feels springy when gently pressed.

* Remove from the oven and immediately turn out on to a sheet of baking paper. Leave to cool for a few moments then carefully peel off the original baking paper.

* Make the syllabub. In a large bowl, mix the lemon zest and juice and honey, stirring until the honey has dissolved. Add the cold cream then whisk until incorporated but still slightly loose.

* Spread the cream over the cooled meringue sponge, leaving about 2.5cm free around the edge. Cover with the raspberries and blueberries, then carefully roll up the meringue using the baking paper to help you. Chill until ready to serve. Just before serving, dust with icing sugar.

Pistachio & Fruit Simnel Cake

LYNN HILL

A traditional Simnel cake has a thin layer of marzipan baked into the centre and is decorated with a circle of marzipan on top and 11 balls of marzipan to represent Jesus' disciples. This cake is a little different because it has all the marzipan balls baked within the cake! It also has the unusual addition of pistachios (and adorable Easter chicks!).

SERVES 12

100g dried cranberries
100g glacé cherries
150g sultanas
150g raisins
50g mixed citrus peel
175g soft light brown sugar
140g butter, diced
250ml tropical citrus juice
2 eggs, beaten
50g pistachio nuts, chopped
300g plain flour
2 tsp baking powder
1 tsp mixed spice
1 tsp cinnamon
250g golden marzipan

Topping:
3 tbsp apricot jam
200g golden marzipan

* Preheat the oven to 170°C/fan 150°C/gas mark 3½. Grease and line a 20cm round, springform cake tin.

* Place all the dried fruits, mixed peel, sugar, butter and juice in a large pan. Bring to a simmer slowly, to melt the butter and sugar, then simmer for 10 minutes on a low heat. Remove from the heat, transfer to a large bowl and leave to cool.

* Once cooled, add the eggs and pistachio nuts and stir until well combined. Add the flour, baking powder and spices and mix until thoroughly combined.

* Divide the marzipan into 11 pieces and shape into balls. Spoon just less than half the cake mixture into the tin and arrange the marzipan balls evenly around the mixture taking care not to let it touch the sides of the tin. Spoon the remainder of the cake mixture on top and smooth out.

* Bake the cake in the bottom of the oven for 1 hour or until a skewer inserted into the centre comes out clean. Leave the cake in the tin to cool completely.

* For the topping, gently warm the jam in a small saucepan. Take 50g of the marzipan and roll it into a large ball, then roll out the remainder and cut out a circle the same diameter as the cake. Cover the top of the cake with warm jam and place the circle of marzipan on top. Place your large ball of marzipan in the middle, using a little jam to help stick it down. Decorate the cake as wished.

Happy Easter

Easter Bun Cake

KAY CUSHNIE

This Jamaican alternative to the English hot cross bun is filled with fruit, spices and stout (which acts as a raising agent). In Jamaica this is traditionally served with a slice of cheese and a cup of tea. The cake will keep for up to four days if stored in an airtight container, but Kay says that in her household it is normally eaten in two!

SERVES 10–12 (OR 5 HUNGRY JAMAICANS)

400g self-raising flour

4 tsp baking powder

175g soft dark brown sugar or dark muscovado sugar

100g caster sugar, plus 4 tbsp for the glaze

½ tsp ground allspice

1 tsp freshly grated nutmeg

1½ tsp ground cinnamon

1½ tsp ground ginger

pinch of salt

200g mixture of raisins, sultanas, cherries (or dried fruit of your choice)

250ml Guinness (or stout of your choice)

30g butter or margarine, diced

2 tsp vanilla extract

✳ Preheat the oven to 170°C/fan 150°C/gas mark 3½. Grease and line a 900g loaf tin.

✳ Sift the flour and baking powder into a large mixing bowl, add the sugars (reserving the quantity for the glaze), spices and salt and mix well. Add the mixed fruit and continue to mix until well combined. Make a well in the centre of the dry mixture.

✳ Pour the Guinness into a saucepan, add the butter and heat gently to melt, stirring. It should be lukewarm. Pour into the well in the centre of the dry mixture, add the vanilla extract and mix well until thoroughly combined.

✳ Transfer the mixture into the tin and smooth the top. Bake for 1¼ hours, until a skewer inserted into the centre comes out clean. Leave to cool in the tin for 10 minutes, then turn out on to a wire rack to cool completely.

✳ To make the glaze, put the remaining four tablespoons of caster sugar into a small saucepan with three tablespoons of water and heat gently, stirring, until the sugar dissolves. Bring to a simmer, then remove from the heat. Brush the warm glaze over the top of the bun.

Pink Champagne Anniversary Cake

SARAH OLLINGTON

Champagne is twice the star of the show in this rich, decadent cake, which is perfect for anniversaries. The sponge is soaked for several hours in a pink champagne syrup, then filled with a delicious pink champagne buttercream and white chocolate ganache, and finally smothered in more of that luxurious buttercream. Cava or Prosecco also work well as cheaper, although less intensely flavoured alternatives to champagne. Serve with a flute of bubbly on the side!

SERVES 12

175g butter, softened
175g caster sugar
3 large eggs
250g self-raising flour
a couple of drops of red food
    colouring
2–3 tbsp milk
grated zest of 1 lemon

Champagne Syrup:
85g granulated sugar
½ tsp vanilla extract
120ml pink champagne

Champagne Buttercream:
225g butter, softened
450g icing sugar
½ tsp vanilla extract
3–4 tbsp pink champagne
    or cava
a couple of drops of red food
    colouring

White Chocolate Ganache:
420g good-quality white
    chocolate (Belgian if
    possible), finely chopped
200ml double cream

✳ Preheat the oven to 200°C/fan 180°C/gas mark 6. Grease and line an 18cm round, springform cake tin.

✳ Beat the butter and sugar using a wooden spoon or electric mixer until light and fluffy. Add the eggs one at a time, beating well after each addition, and adding a tablespoon of the flour with the final egg to help prevent curdling. Stir in the red food colouring. Sift in the remaining flour and fold gently until thoroughly combined. Stir in the milk until you reach a dropping consistency, then add the lemon zest.

✳ Spoon the mixture into the tin, spreading it evenly. Bake for about 40 minutes or until a skewer inserted into the centre comes out clean. Leave to cool in the tin for 10 minutes, then turn out on to a wire rack to cool completely.

✳ Meanwhile, make the champagne soaking syrup. Combine the sugar, vanilla and 175ml water in a small saucepan and heat gently until the sugar has dissolved. When the syrup is warm, stir in the pink champagne, then remove from the heat and set aside.

✳ When the cake is cool, pour 100–150ml of the champagne syrup over the cake and leave to soak for a couple of hours.

✳ Make the champagne buttercream. Beat the butter and icing sugar until throughly combined. Add the vanilla and champagne and mix again until incorporated. Add the red food colouring and mix until the colour is uniform.

✳ Finally, make the white chocolate ganache. Put the white chocolate into a heatproof mixing bowl and set aside. Heat the cream in a small saucepan until just simmering but not boiling (boiling it will curdle your chocolate). Pour the cream over the chocolate and stir until the chocolate is melted and smooth. Set aside to cool.

CONTINUED ➡

* To assemble, cut your cake into three layers using a large serrated knife. Place a large dollop of buttercream on to one layer and spread evenly with a palette knife to about 5mm thick. Place a big dollop of ganache on top of the buttercream and gently spread out, then cover with a second cake layer.

* Repeat the process, then place the final cake layer on top. Using the palette knife, cover the top and sides of the cake with a thin layer of buttercream (the 'crumb coat', see Tip on page 30). Leave to chill in the fridge for about an hour, until firm and set, then use the remaining buttercream to cover the top and sides.

Father's Day Spiced Ale Cake

DEB CONNOR

What better treat for Father's Day than a cake made with his favourite beer?! This is a quick recipe to make and the cake has a dense texture and a comforting, spicy aftertaste. You can adjust the amount of spices to suit. It's delicious toasted and drizzled with honey for breakfast.

SERVES 12

350ml light ale
100g sultanas
2 tbsp honey (clear or set) or agave nectar
200g dark muscovado sugar
400g wholemeal flour
1 tsp bicarbonate of soda
1 tsp ground cinnamon
½ tsp ground cloves

* Mix the ale with the sultanas and leave for a couple of hours for the fruit to plump up a little and absorb some of the ale's flavour.

* Preheat the oven to 190°C/fan 170°C/gas mark 5. Grease and line the base and sides of a 900g loaf tin leaving a little of the paper above the rim to allow for any rising.

* Gently warm the honey and add to the ale and sultanas along with the sugar, stirring until all the sugar has dissolved.

* Mix all the dry ingredients together in a bowl and then pour in the ale mixture. Stir until thoroughly combined into a thick batter.

* Pour the mixture into the tin, spreading it evenly. Bake in the oven for 40–45 minutes, until a skewer inserted into the centre comes out clean. Leave to cool in the tin completely before turning out. This cake can be kept in an airtight container for up to a week.

Italian Cream Wedding Cake

JULIE CARNEY

In Italy, this divine three-layer cake is often served as a wedding cake, and it is fancy enough to suit all types of special occasion, especially when decorated with handmade chocolate leaves (see Tip) or sugar flowers. The buttermilk gives the sponge a lovely soft texture and a pleasant tang.

SERVES 15–20

225g butter, softened
400g caster sugar
5 large eggs, separated
250g plain flour
1 tsp bicarbonate of soda
355ml buttermilk
100g chopped almonds
100g chopped hazelnuts
75g desiccated coconut

Frosting:
230g butter, softened
450g cream cheese
2 tsp vanilla extract
840g icing sugar
30g nuts (such as a mixture of almonds and hazelnuts), chopped

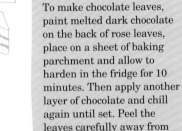

TIP

To make chocolate leaves, paint melted dark chocolate on the back of rose leaves, place on a sheet of baking parchment and allow to harden in the fridge for 10 minutes. Then apply another layer of chocolate and chill again until set. Peel the leaves carefully away from the chocolate and they're ready to use.

* Preheat the oven to 195°C/fan 175°C/gas mark 5½. Grease and line three 20cm round sandwich tins.

* Beat the butter and sugar using a wooden spoon or electric mixer until light and fluffy. Add the egg yolks one at a time, beating well after each addition, and adding a tablespoon of the flour with the final egg to help prevent curdling.

* Sift the flour and bicarbonate of soda together and add this in small amounts, alternating it with the buttermilk. Stir in the nuts and coconut.

* Beat the egg whites until stiff peaks form and fold into the batter mix. Pour the mixture into the tin, spreading it evenly. Bake for 25–30 minutes or until a skewer inserted into the centre comes out clean.

* Leave the cakes to cool in the tins for 10 minutes before turning out on to a wire rack to cool completely. Take care turning the cakes out as they are very light and delicate and will tear easily.

* For the frosting, beat the butter in a bowl until smooth. Add the cream cheese and vanilla extract and mix until combined, then sift in the icing sugar at intervals until it is all combined. Spread a layer on to each of the cooled cakes, then pile them up and spread the remainder all over the top and sides. Decorate the sides or top with the chopped nuts and with chocolate leaves, if you wish (see Tip).

'Trick or Treat' Tuck Shop Cake

WITH LEMON SHERBET BUTTERCREAM

JO CHRISTY

This stunning cake came about when Jo accidentally dropped some M&Ms into her batter. It resulted in a multi-coloured marbled sponge, which she topped off with a fizzy sherbet buttercream. Don't hold back with the decorations ... but be warned that your kids probably will need holding back!

SERVES 10–12

200g softened butter
   or soft margarine
200g caster sugar
4 eggs, beaten
200g self-raising flour, sifted
1 tsp baking powder
about 2 tbsp milk
1 x 125g pack of chocolate
   M&Ms, crushed
sweets, such as dolly mixture
   and jelly babies, to decorate

Sherbet Buttercream:

400g butter, at room
   temperature, diced
560g icing sugar
1 x 23g packet sherbet
   dip dab, sherbet only

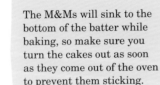

The M&Ms will sink to the bottom of the batter while baking, so make sure you turn the cakes out as soon as they come out of the oven to prevent them sticking.

* Preheat the oven to 180°C/fan 160°C/gas mark 4. Grease and line two 20cm round sandwich tins.

* Beat the butter and sugar using a wooden spoon or electric mixer until light and fluffy. Add the eggs one at a time, beating well after each addition, and adding a tablespoon of the flour with the final egg to help prevent curdling. Fold in the remaining flour and baking powder until thoroughly combined. Stir in enough milk as you need to reach a soft dropping consistency. Mix in the M&Ms until well combined.

* Divide the mixture between the tins, spreading it evenly and smoothing the top with a spatula or the back of a spoon. Bake for 20 minutes or until golden on top and the top of the cake springs back when gently pressed. Turn out on to a wire rack and leave to cool completely.

* To make the buttercream, beat the butter to soften it, then sift in the icing sugar, a little at a time, mixing well (preferably with an electric mixer) to combine. Add the sherbet and mix until thoroughly combined and the buttercream is a firm piping consistency.

* Once the sponges are completely cool, transfer the buttercream to a piping bag fitted with a large star-shaped nozzle. Pipe half the mix on to the bottom layer in swirls about 2cm wide and 2cm tall, starting from the outside and working into the middle in a spiral. This will give the second sponge some lift when it is placed on top.

* Use the remaining buttercream to pipe a circle of swirls around the outside edge of the top of the cake, then decorate with the dolly mixture and jelly babies, leaving a section of the sponge visible. The beautiful marbled effect of the sponge can then be shown off to your admirers, just peeking out in the middle to entice them.

Harvest Spiced Apple Cake

BECCA LUNDBERG

This is a wonderful, sticky, spiced cake with a caramelised almond and apple topping. The warming autumnal aromas of cardamom, star anise and cinnamon are heavenly. It's a clever way to use up a glut of apples, and it is an ideal cake for the Harvest Festival celebrations or as a Boxing Day treat with a glass of mulled wine. It's equally nice served cold or hot with ice cream.

SERVES 8–10

225g unsalted butter, plus 30g for greasing the tin

30g soft light brown sugar

225g caster sugar

1 tsp vanilla extract

4 eggs

225g self-raising flour

½ tsp baking powder

2–3 tbsp milk

50g flaked almonds

Spiced Apples:

2 cooking apples, such as Bramley, peeled, cored and cut into 1cm slices

200ml orange juice

½ tsp freshly grated nutmeg, plus extra to dust

1 cinnamon stick or 1 tsp ground cinnamom, plus extra to dust

2 star anise (optional)

5 whole cardamom pods (optional)

30g soft light brown sugar

* Start by preparing the spiced apples. Place the apples in a saucepan with the orange juice, spices and sugar. Cover with a lid and heat gently until the apple is soft but not breaking up. Remove from the heat and leave with the lid on to cool and to let the spices infuse further.

* Preheat the oven to 200°C/fan 180°C/gas mark 6. Line the base of a 23cm round, springform cake tin and grease the paper and sides of the tin thickly with the 30g butter. Sprinkle the base with the brown sugar. Lightly dust with some cinnamon and freshly grated nutmeg.

* Beat the butter and caster sugar using a wooden spoon or electric mixer until light and fluffy, then add the vanilla. Add the eggs one at a time, beating well after each addition, and adding a tablespoon of the flour with the final egg to help prevent curdling. Sift in the flour and baking powder and fold in. Stir in enough of the milk to give a soft dropping consistency.

* Strain the apples and remove the cinnamon stick, star anise and cardamom pods. Scatter the flaked almonds over the base of the tin, then place the apples on top. Cover with the cake mixture.

* Bake in the oven for about 50 minutes, until the cake is springy to the touch and a skewer inserted into the centre comes out clean. Allow the cake to cool in the tin for 1 hour, then turn out on to a plate or cake stand so that the nuts are on top.

Thanksgiving Pumpkin Cake

VANESSA B. DRAPER

This variation on pumpkin pie is an easy recipe that requires minimal work, and the combination of pumpkin, spices and maple syrup creates a sensational, comforting aroma. You needn't wait for Thanksgiving though – it's delicious served warm with a nice mug of coffee during those chilly autumn months. This will keep in the fridge for up to a week if covered with cling film and also freezes very well without the frosting.

SERVES 8–10

250g plain flour

100g caster sugar

100g soft dark brown sugar

1 tsp baking powder

1 tsp ground cinnamon, plus extra to dust (optional)

¼ tsp freshly grated nutmeg

¼ tsp ginger

4 tbsp maple syrup

½ tsp salt

250g mashed pumpkin or canned pumpkin purée

120ml vegetable oil

2 eggs

pecan nuts, crushed, to decorate (optional)

Cream Cheese Frosting:

55g butter, softened, or margarine

100g cream cheese

½ tsp vanilla extract

100g icing sugar

* Preheat the oven to 200°C/fan 180°C/gas mark 6. Grease and line a shallow 20cm square cake tin.

* Combine the flour, sugars, baking powder, cinnamon, nutmeg, ginger, maple syrup and salt in a large mixing bowl, then add the pumpkin, oil and eggs and mix until combined.

* Pour the mixture into the tin and bake for 25–30 minutes, or until a skewer inserted in the centre comes out clean. Leave in the tin for 10 minutes, then turn out on to a wire rack to cool completely.

* Make the frosting. Beat the butter until smooth, then add the cream cheese and mix until combined. Mix in the vanilla then gradually sift in the icing sugar and beat until light and fluffy.

* When the cake is cool, spread the icing over the top with a spatula. Decorate with a dusting of ground cinnamon along with some crushed pecans, if you like.

Rich Celebration Fruit Cake

ANNIE FOLEY

A rich fruit cake is hard to beat for Christmas, weddings and christenings. Ideally, make it 4–6 weeks in advance and feed it regularly with plenty of brandy, though Annie once began this process only two weeks ahead of an event and her cake still tasted as though it had been fed for weeks. Adding the thin layer of marzipan under the fondant icing gives a smooth and professional-looking finish.

SERVES 24

225g sultanas

225g raisins

200g currants

175g glacé cherries, rinsed, drained and roughly chopped

150g dried apricots, roughly chopped

125g dried figs, roughly chopped

150ml brandy

300g grated carrots

2 large sharp eating apples, such as Granny Smith, peeled and grated

75g flaked almonds

75g walnuts, roughly chopped

350g plain flour

½ tsp mixed spice

½ tsp cinnamon

½ tsp freshly grated nutmeg

275g butter, softened

275g soft dark brown sugar

grated zest of 2 oranges

grated zest of 1 lemon

5 large eggs, lightly beaten

3 tbsp black treacle

INGREDIENTS
CONTINUED OVERLEAF

* The night before you wish to bake, put all the dried fruit into a large bowl and add around eight tablespoons of the brandy. Stir well, cover with a clean cloth and leave overnight.

* The next day, preheat the oven to 170°C/fan 150°C/gas mark 3½. Grease and line a 23cm square cake tin with a double layer of baking paper.

* Add the carrots, apples, almonds and walnuts to the fruit mixture. In a separate bowl, sift together the flour and spices and set aside.

* In a large bowl, beat the butter, sugar and citrus zests using a wooden spoon or electric mixer until light and fluffy. Add the eggs one at a time, beating well after each addition, and adding a tablespoon of the flour with the final egg to help prevent curdling. Stir in the treacle, then very gently fold in the flour mixture. Add the fruit and stir well. Spoon into the prepared tin and smooth the top.

* Cut two square sheets of greaseproof paper the same size as your tin; make a small hole in the centre and place on top of the cake. Tie two sheets of brown paper around the tin cut to size and secure with string, then stand the tin on two sheets of brown paper and place in the centre of the oven – this will prevent the cake from burning.

* Bake for about 2½ hours or until a skewer inserted into the centre comes out clean. As soon as it's out of the oven, leave the cake in the tin and make holes all over the top with the skewer. Brush with some of the remaining brandy and immediately wrap the whole cake in foil, then leave to cool completely – this seals in all the moisture.

* Turn out of the tin and wrap in greaseproof paper feeding it about once a week for 4–6 weeks, until ready to decorate.

CONTINUED ➡

Rich Celebration Fruit Cake

Decoration:

1–2 tbsp apricot jam, sieved, boiled and allowed to cool

icing sugar, to roll out

1.45kg golden marzipan

1kg ready-to-roll white sugarpaste

a selection of food colouring pastes (according to preference)

✳ To decorate, place the cake on a cake board, using a little sugarpaste to secure it. Fill any holes in the cake with small pieces of marzipan, then brush with the boiled jam.

✳ Dust a surface with icing sugar and roll out the marzipan until it is about 5mm thick and wide enough to cover the whole cake. Then pick it up over a rolling pin and carefully drape it over the cake. Press it gently down the sides of the cake, smoothing out any bumps, then cut off any excess and cover the cake with a clean tea towel. Leave for approximately two days to dry out.

✳ Dust a surface with icing sugar and roll out the sugarpaste, turning it frequently and using lots of icing sugar to roll it out until it is around 3–4mm thick and wide enough to cover the whole cake. Brush the cake with boiled water, then pick up the sugarpaste over a rolling pin and carefully drape it over the cake. Press it gently down the sides of the cake, smoothing out any bumps, then cut off any excess. Using a small pastry brush, carefully brush off any excess icing sugar.

✳ Colour the sugarpaste trimmings and use them to make decorations, such as a robin, snowman or Christmas tree. Leave the cake to dry for at least a day before serving.

Christmas Honey Cake

KAREN JEFFERSON

Freshly brewed coffee, vanilla, whisky and pungent spices combine to make this cake ideal as a lighter alternative to the traditional Christmas cake. What a warm, comfy, armchair moment of self-indulgence! The use of a different-flavoured honey can make quite a difference to the final taste. Try building up the glaze in multiple coats for a more intense taste and a lovely layered visual effect.

SERVES 15–20

235ml vegetable oil
235ml clear heather honey
150g golden caster sugar
110g dark brown sugar
3 large eggs
1 tsp vanilla extract
235ml strong coffee
120ml freshly squeezed
    orange juice
60ml whisky
440g plain flour
1 tbsp baking powder
1 tsp bicarbonate of soda
½ tsp salt
4 tsp ground cinnamon
1 tsp ground cloves
1 tsp freshly grated nutmeg
1 tsp ground ginger

Glaze (optional):
5 tbsp clear honey
2 tbsp freshly squeezed
    orange juice

* Preheat the oven to 160°C/fan 140°C/gas mark 3. Grease and flour a 2.5–3-litre bundt tin.

* In a bowl, whisk together the oil, honey, sugars, eggs, vanilla, coffee, orange juice and whisky. Whisk in the flour, baking powder, bicarbonate of soda, salt and spices until thoroughly combined.

* Pour the batter into the tin, spreading it evenly.

* Bake on the top shelf of the oven for about 1 hour, until the cake is golden brown and a skewer inserted into the centre comes out with just a few crumbs sticking to it. Leave to cool in the tin for a few minutes then turn out on to a wire rack and leave to cool completely.

* If you wish to glaze the cake, gently heat the honey and orange juice in a small saucepan and brush the warm glaze over the cake. Build it up in three or four layers, leaving each layer to dry for a few minutes before applying the next. You can also make small holes in the cake to allow the glaze to soak in more. The cake can be eaten warm or left to cool completely; it tastes especially good the next day.

Hogmanay Dundee Cake

DOUSED IN WHISKY

KAREN S. BURNS-BOOTH

This cake contains a good slug of Scotch whisky, which plumps up the fruit and adds a delicious smoky flavour. Bake in advance if you can, and feed with whisky for several weeks. Almonds and glacé cherries add the perfect festive finish.

SERVES 8–12

300g luxury dried mixed fruit
50g mixed peel
grated zest and juice
   of 1 clementine
100g butter, diced
100g soft light brown sugar
1 large egg, beaten
25g ground almonds
1 tsp mixed spice
200g self-raising flour, sifted
25g whole blanched almonds
Scotch whisky, to feed the cake
a few glacé cherries,
   to decorate (optional)

TIP

You can adapt this recipe to make three mini cakes to give as Christmas gifts – if you don't have small baking tins, simply use leftover syrup-sponge tins (these are the ideal size), or baked bean tins. Reduce the cooking time to 50–55 minutes.

＊ Preheat the oven to 150°C/fan 130°C/gas mark 2. Grease and line an 18cm round, springform cake tin.

＊ Place the dried fruit, peel, clementine zest and juice, butter, sugar and 150ml water in a saucepan. Bring to a simmer, cover and simmer gently over a low heat for 20 minutes.

＊ Remove from the heat and leave to cool, then add the beaten egg, ground almonds, mixed spice and sifted flour. Mix well, then pour into the tin, spreading the mixture evenly. Arrange the blanched almonds on the top of the cake, then shake the tin gently to level the mixture.

＊ Bake for about 1 hour, until a skewer inserted into the centre comes out clean. Leave the cake to cool in the tin for 10 minutes before turning out on to a wire rack to cool completely.

＊ Once completely cool, pierce the base of the cake all over with a knitting needle or a skewer and feed the cake with a few tablespoons of whisky. Feed the cake with whisky about 2–3 times a week for 2–3 weeks before decorating the top with the glacé cherries, if using.

This is where Clandestine Cake Club members really pull out all the stops! Get ready for butterflies, rainbows and enchanted forests… In this sensational chapter, you will find a fabulous collection of wonderfully creative cakes that will capture your imagination and make you smile.

These are perfect party pieces, fit for a crowd and bound to impress your friends. Some of these recipes will stretch your baking skills more than others, but with a little careful planning and plenty of time set aside, they can all be achieved and enjoyed by anyone. Even if they turn out a little bit wonky, there will be no doubt about the effort you put in to make a special and delicious creation.

Creative
Cakes

Strawberry Butterfly Bundt

RACHEL MCGRATH

Perfect for a girly birthday party or afternoon tea in the sun, this pretty sponge cake is incredibly light and has a subtle flavour. It is made in a specialist bundt tin, available from good online baking suppliers. Make sure not to fill the tin more than three-quarters full and always test with a skewer to check the sponge is baked through.

SERVES 12

225g butter, softened

450g golden caster sugar

4 eggs

350g plain flour

½ tsp bicarbonate of soda

½ tsp salt

350g good-quality thick strawberry yoghurt (one with plenty of fruit in it for flavour)

1 tsp vanilla extract

½ tsp strawberry essence (optional)

coloured glacé icing (see page 248), to decorate (optional)

Adapt this recipe to suit your taste by using a different flavoured fruit yoghurt and replacing the strawberry essence with your preferred fruit essence or extract.

* Preheat the oven to 170°C/fan 150°C/gas mark 3½. Grease and flour a 2.5–3-litre butterfly-shaped bundt tin.

* Beat the butter and sugar using a wooden spoon or electric mixer until soft. Add the eggs one at a time, beating well after each addition, and adding a tablespoon of the flour with the final egg to help prevent curdling.

* In a separate bowl, combine the remaining flour, bicarbonate of soda and salt. Pour the yoghurt, vanilla and strawberry essence (if using) into the egg mixture and mix well.

* Sift in the flour in two halves. Mix in slowly until all the flour has disappeared. Over-mixing at this stage will make a dense cake and create air channels in the batter, which can ruin the shape of a decorative bundt.

* Pour the mixture into the tin. Bake in the centre of the oven for about 1¼ hours or until a skewer inserted into the centre comes out clean. It's stable from about an hour in if you want to check it or turn it.

* Leave the cake to cool completely before removing from the tin. Serve either plain, dusted with icing sugar or decorated with coloured glacé icing (see page 248) as shown in the photo.

Coffee 'Cup' Cake

CHARLIE SCOTT KING

Your guests might double-take when they see this cake, thinking it truly is a giant cup of coffee! Even the giant cup and handle are edible, as they are made from icing. Charlie created this to get around the rule that says cupcakes aren't allowed at CCC – but a 'cup' cake certainly is! The secret to the shape is to make it in a pudding basin. You can add a frothy 'cappuccino' topping, or leave it plain as an espresso.

SERVES 8–10

200g butter, softened

200g caster sugar

4 large eggs

225g self-raising flour

75ml very strong espresso coffee or Camp coffee essence

Icing:

50g apricot jam, warmed and sieved

500g ready-to-roll white sugarpaste

Cappuccino Topping (optional):

50g softened butter or margarine

about 200g icing sugar

50ml very strong espresso coffee or Camp coffee essence

cocoa powder, to dust

⁕ Preheat the oven to 190°C/fan 170°C/gas mark 5. Grease a 1.2-litre Pyrex pudding bowl. Line the base with a circle of baking paper, then line the sides with strips of the paper.

⁕ Beat the butter and sugar using a wooden spoon or electric mixer until soft. Add the eggs one at a time, beating well, and adding a tablespoon of the flour with the final egg to help prevent curdling, then add 25ml of the coffee. Fold in the flour using a large metal spoon, until combined.

⁕ Spoon the mixture into the dish. Bake in the oven for 45 minutes–1 hour, until a skewer inserted into the centre comes out clean. Leave to cool in the bowl for 15 minutes, then carefully flip out on to a wire rack and remove all the baking paper. Leave to cool for 1–1½ hours.

⁕ To ice the cake, place on the table with the domed side up. Using a pastry brush, brush on the warmed jam. Sift a little icing sugar over a clean surface and knead the sugarpaste until soft and smooth. Set aside 50g of the sugarpaste for later. Roll out the rest to 5mm thick and large enough to cover the cake. Pick up the sugarpaste over a rolling pin, carefully drape over the cake, and smooth down with your hands.

⁕ Cut off the excess round the base, leaving about 1.5cm around the edge – this will form the rim of the 'cup'. Turn the cake the other way up and place on a serving plate. Fold the excess icing in at the top to make a rim.

⁕ Using a teaspoon, feed the cake with the remaining 50ml of the coffee, being careful not to get any on the sugarpaste. Use the reserved 50g of sugarpaste to make the handle. Secure using cocktail sticks or jam.

⁕ For a frothy cappuccino topping, beat the butter or margarine and half the icing sugar, then gradually beat in the coffee. Add enough of the remaining icing sugar to give a good coffee colour; the topping should be just thick enough to hold its shape. Spoon over the cake and swirl gently so that it looks like a freshly made cappuccino. Dust with cocoa powder.

Toffee Shock Cake

JULIA ENGLAND

Created for a fairytale-themed event, this magical cake has four different-flavoured layers, a caramel filling, and fudge, toffee and popping candy on top! You will only need a small slice of this rich creation, but it can be stored for up to three days, so you can keep coming back for more.

SERVES 16–20

Vanilla & Chocolate Layers:

225g butter, very soft

225g caster sugar

175g self-raising flour

85g ground almonds

1 tsp baking powder

3 eggs

150ml natural yoghurt

1 tsp vanilla extract

5 tbsp cocoa powder

Caramel & Choco-Caramel Layers:

225g butter, very soft

175g light muscovado sugar

50g dark muscovado sugar

175g self-raising flour

85g ground almonds

1 tsp baking powder

3 eggs

150ml natural yoghurt

1 tsp vanilla extract

1 tbsp cocoa powder

Fudge Icing:

150ml evaporated milk

150g granulated sugar

225g good-quality dark chocolate

75g butter

Filling & Decoration:

400g canned caramel

fudge pieces, toffees and popping candy, to decorate

* Preheat the oven to 180°C/fan 160°C/gas mark 4. Grease and line two 20cm round sandwich tins.

* For the vanilla and chocolate sponge layers, mix all the ingredients apart from the cocoa, until you have a smooth batter. Put half the mixture into a second bowl and stir the cocoa into this batch. Pour the batters into the two prepared tins and spread evenly. Bake for 20–25 minutes, until the cakes are springy to the touch and a skewer inserted into the centre comes out clean. Leave to cool in the tins for 10 minutes, then turn out on to a wire rack to cool completely.

* For the caramel and choco-caramel layers, mix all the ingredients, again leaving out the cocoa, to a smooth batter, then split the mixture in half and add the cocoa to one batch. Bake and cool as above.

* Meanwhile, make the fudge icing. Put the evaporated milk and sugar in a small saucepan and heat gently to dissolve the sugar. Bring to the boil and simmer for 2–3 minutes, without stirring, then remove from the heat. Stir in the chocolate until completely melted, then add the butter and stir until you have a glossy fudge. Transfer to a bowl and set aside to cool completely.

* Once the cakes are cool, spread a third of the canned caramel over your chosen base cake and top with the next sponge layer. Repeat with the rest of the canned caramel and sponge layers, arranging the layers in whichever order you like.

* Using a palette knife, spread the fudge icing over the top and sides of the whole cake, then scatter over the fudge and toffee pieces. Only place the popping candy on the cake when you're ready to serve otherwise all the pop will crackle and fizz with no appreciation from the cake eaters. The cake can be stored in a cool place in an airtight container for up to three days.

Pina Colada Cake

NICOLA LATHAM

With its dark rum and fresh pineapple, you'll find a taste of the sunny tropics in this mouth-watering and richly flavoured cake, inspired by one of the world's most popular holiday cocktails! Allow plenty of time at the start for the pineapple to absorb all the rum and brown sugar before you proceed to use it in the method.

SERVES 10–12

½ medium fresh pineapple, peeled, roughly chopped

2 tbsp dark rum (preferably spiced)

1 tbsp soft light brown sugar

½ x 340g jar pineapple jam or conserve (optional, for a sweeter filling)

225g butter, softened

225g caster sugar

4 eggs

225g self-raising flour

25g desiccated coconut, toasted, to decorate

grated zest of ½ lime, to decorate

Malibu Frosting:

200g cream cheese

125g icing sugar

1 tbsp Malibu

100ml double cream

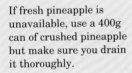

TIP

If fresh pineapple is unavailable, use a 400g can of crushed pineapple but make sure you drain it thoroughly.

* Place the pineapple in a bowl with the rum and brown sugar and leave to soak for at least 6 hours, preferably overnight. Strain the fruit.

* Preheat the oven to 200°C/fan 180°C/gas mark 6. Grease and line two 18cm round sandwich tins.

* Roughly mash the pineapple with a fork to break it down – it should be a chunky pulp but you should be able to spread it. Take care not to overwork or it will be runny. Mix with the pineapple jam, if using.

* Beat the butter and sugar using a wooden spoon or electric mixer until light and fluffy. Add the eggs one at a time, beating well after each addition, and adding a tablespoon of the flour with the final egg to help prevent curdling. Sift the remaining flour into the mixture in two batches and fold in gently with a large metal spoon.

* Transfer to the tins and smooth the tops. Bake for about 25 minutes or until a skewer inserted into the centre comes out clean. Leave to cool in the tins for 10 minutes, then turn out on to a wire rack to cool completely.

* To make the frosting, beat the cream cheese, icing sugar and Malibu until smooth. Whisk in the double cream until the mixture is firm.

* To assemble, spread two-thirds of the frosting on to one cake, followed by the pineapple mixture. Cover with the other cake and spread the remaining frosting over the top. Decorate with the toasted coconut and lime zest.

PHOTO, FROM LEFT: PINA COLADA CAKE; SHIRLEY TEMPLE MOCKTAIL CAKE

Shirley Temple Mocktail Cake

NELLY RITCHIE

Inspired by the non-alcoholic cocktail said to have been created for a young Shirley Temple in the 1930s, this cake was devised for a 'Baking with Beverages' themed event. With its fizzy ginger ale sponge, zingy lime curd and Maraschino-cherry buttercream, it will be quickly devoured by anyone with a sweet tooth! See photo on previous page.

SERVES 16

240g plain flour
280g caster sugar
80g butter, soft
1 tbsp baking powder
large pinch of salt
1 tsp ground ginger
1 tsp mixed spice
220ml ginger ale
2 large eggs
1½ tsp vanilla extract
grated zest of 1 lime, plus
   2 tsp of juice
cocktail cherries, to decorate

Lime Curd:

60ml lime juice
135g caster sugar
25g cornflour
2 egg yolks
1 tbsp butter
grated zest of ½ lime

Cherry Buttercream:

200g butter, softened
1–2 tbsp cherry syrup from
   a jar of cocktail cherries
400g icing sugar
pink food colouring
about 1 tbsp milk

* Preheat the oven to 200°C/fan 180°C/gas mark 6. Grease and line a 20cm round, springform cake tin.

* Beat the flour, sugar, butter, baking powder, salt and spices using a wooden spoon or electric mixer until everything is combined and the mixture resembles breadcrumbs. Gradually add half the ginger ale and beat until just incorporated.

* In a separate bowl, whisk together the eggs, vanilla extract, lime zest and juice and remaining ginger ale, then pour into the flour mixture and beat until well combined. Pour into the tin and bake for 1 hour or until a skewer inserted into the centre comes out clean. Leave to cool in the tin for 10 minutes, then turn out on to a wire rack.

* Once cool, cut the cake in half horizontally using a large serrated knife and either level the top or turn the cake upside down so that the flat surface is on top.

* Make the lime curd. Put all the ingredients into a saucepan with 100ml water and place over a medium heat. Whisk continuously until it starts to thicken then remove from the heat and continue whisking until you have a thick curd. If you want a stronger green colour you can add food colouring too. Set aside to cool then spread the curd on top of one cake layer and sandwich with the other layer.

* Make the buttercream. Beat the butter and cherry syrup together until combined, then gradually sift in the icing sugar until well mixed. Add the desired amount of pink food colouring and if the mixture is too stiff gradually add a little milk to soften it slightly.

* Using a palette knife, cover the top and sides of the cake with a thin layer of buttercream (the 'crumb coat', see Tip on page 30) then chill in the fridge for 30 minutes, until it has set. Apply a second, thicker coat of buttercream with a palette knife, dipping the knife in boiling water to give your cake a clean finish. Dot with cherries to decorate.

Giant Lemon Fondant Fancy

JINI MULUKUTLA

Who doesn't love Mr Kipling's famous fondant fancies? This larger-than-life version will make your friends' eyes pop out of their heads! It does need a little planning, so make sure you have all your tools and ingredients ready before you start, and set aside time for the sponge base to cool overnight. If you're feeling really ambitious, why not create your own strawberry and chocolate variations to complete the set?

SERVES 8–10

160g butter, softened
190g caster sugar
3 large eggs
190g self-raising flour
pinch of salt
1 tsp lemon extract
grated zest of 1 lemon
juice of ½ lemon
about 6 tbsp good-quality
  lemon curd, to fill

Lemon Buttercream:
40g butter, softened
90g icing sugar
2 tsp lemon juice

Icing & Decoration:
yellow gel food colouring
  (not liquid)
500g ready-to-roll white
  sugarpaste
500g marzipan (optional, but
  gives the cake a smoother
  finish)
icing sugar, to roll out
a little ready-to-use royal icing
  (or make a quick glacé icing –
  see page 248)

* Preheat the oven to 180°C/fan 160°C/gas mark 4. Grease and line a deep 15cm square cake tin.

* Beat the butter and sugar using a wooden spoon or electric mixer until light and fluffy. Add the eggs one at a time, beating well after each addition, and adding a tablespoon of the flour with the final egg to help prevent curdling. Fold in the remaining flour and salt. Add the lemon extract, lemon zest and juice and fold in well.

* Place the mixture in the prepared tin and bake in the oven for about 40 minutes, until a skewer inserted into the centre comes out clean. Leave to cool in the tin for 10 minutes, then turn out on to a wire rack and leave to cool completely.

* The next day, make the buttercream. Beat the butter, icing sugar and lemon juice until light and fluffy. Turn the buttercream out on to a square of cling film, pull the cling film up over it and twist the ends together so the buttercream is firmly wrapped. Shape the buttercream into a smooth ball with your hands – if you have a suitable wine glass you could put the buttercream in it at this stage to help mould it into a smooth round shape. Chill until firm.

* Cut the cake in half horizontally and fill with a generous layer of the lemon curd. Brush the rest of the lemon curd over the cake's top and sides. Chill until firm. Unwrap the buttercream and place it on top of the cake, in the centre. Place the cake on a raised board or turntable.

* For the icing, mix the food colouring into the sugarpaste and knead well to spread the colour evenly.

CONTINUED ➡

* If you are using the marzipan, dust a surface with icing sugar and roll it out to about 3mm thick. Lift it up over the rolling pin and carefully drape it over the cake, shaping it over the mound of buttercream and the edges of the cake with your hands. Smooth out any bumps, then trim off the excess. Chill for several hours or overnight.

* On a work surface dusted with icing sugar, roll out the sugarpaste to 4–5mm thick. Lift it up on the rolling pin and carefully drape it over the cake. Smooth it down and trim off the excess as for the marzipan. Gently rub the sugarpaste with your hands, using a circular motion, to give a smooth finish. Leave to dry for a couple of hours.

* To finish, put a little royal icing or glacé icing in a piping bag fitted with a small plain nozzle (you could also use a squeezy bottle for the glacé icing), and carefully pipe it over the cake in diagonal lines. Leave to set, then transfer the cake to a serving plate or 20cm paper cake liner.

Mocha Hedgehog Cake

HELEN FERGUSON

Harry the Hedgehog is an all-time favourite birthday cake in Helen's household, and is loved by grown-ups and kids alike. Easy to make, this is an excellent opportunity to get children involved in the baking – let them bring Harry to life with Smarties for his nose and eyes and chocolate buttons for his bristles. Just don't take your eyes off him or he might disappear into the garden…!

SERVES 12

170g very soft butter or
    margarine
170g caster sugar
3 large eggs
130g self-raising flour
40g cocoa powder
1 tsp baking powder
2 tsp instant coffee granules
    dissolved in 3 tsp boiling
    water then cooled
3 Smarties or other chocolate
    beans (for nose and eyes)
2 bags of milk chocolate
    buttons, to decorate

Filling & Icing:
150g margarine
2 tsp instant coffee granules
    dissolved in 3 tsp boiling
    water
250g icing sugar
50g cocoa powder

* Preheat the oven to 190°C/fan 170°C/gas mark 5. Grease and line a 20cm round, springform cake tin.

* Put the butter or margarine in a large bowl and add the sugar and eggs. Sift in the flour, cocoa and baking powder. Give everything a stir (to avoid a cloud of flour), then mix together using a hand mixer or wooden spoon. Add the coffee and combine thoroughly.

* Transfer the mixture to the tin, spreading in evenly. Bake for about 35–40 minutes, until a skewer inserted into the centre comes out clean. Leave to cool in the tin for 10 minutes before turning out on to a wire rack to cool completely.

* Make the filling and icing. Beat the margarine until soft, then mix in the coffee. Gradually add the icing sugar and cocoa powder, mixing well until thoroughly combined.

* To assemble, cut the cake in half vertically using a large serrated knife to give you two semicircles. Sandwich the halves together using a quarter of the filling. Using the serrated knife, shave a little off each side to make a more rounded shape. Trim off more right at the front to create a face and nose. This does not have to be perfect as it will be covered.

* Spread the remaining chocolate icing over the cake, filling in the sides with extra icing and shaping the face and nose, smoothing the icing. Use a fork to mark out bristles behind the face, then use the Smarties or other chocolate beans as the nose and eyes. Finally, stick in the chocolate buttons to make taller spikes.

Blue Velvet Cake

CARLA VALENTINE

Carla created this alternative to red velvet cake as a nod to the film of the same name, for an unconventional 'Film Noir' themed club event. The secret to achieving the perfect shade of blue is to add a little bit of purple colouring as well (if you use blue on its own, the sponge will turn out green). Carla's work colleagues will happily testify to how many trial cakes it took for her to find the right shade!

SERVES 12

225g butter, at room temperature
500g golden caster sugar
2 large eggs
15g cocoa powder
blue gel food colouring (ideally 'ice blue')
purple gel food colouring (ideally 'grape')
250g plain flour
1 tsp salt
240ml buttermilk
1 tsp vanilla extract
½ tsp bicarbonate of soda
1 tbsp cider vinegar

Cream Cheese Frosting:
120g butter, softened
230g cream cheese, softened
450g icing sugar

TIP

Use gel or paste colour (available online and now in some of the bigger supermarkets) for the strongest colour.

* Preheat the oven to 195°C/fan 175°C/gas mark 5½. Grease and line two 23cm round, springform cake tins.

* Beat the butter and sugar using a wooden spoon or electric mixer until light and fluffy. Add the eggs one at a time, beating well after each addition, and adding a tablespoon of the flour with the final egg to help prevent curdling. Add the cocoa powder and one teaspoon of blue food colouring and mix well – the batter will become an odd shade of green. Add half a teaspoon of the purple colouring and mix again. If necessary, add more purple until it becomes the right shade of blue.

* Sift the flour and salt together and add this in small amounts, alternating it with the buttermilk. Mix in the vanilla. If at this point the cake is not quite your desired shade of blue, add more purple.

* Mix the bicarbonate of soda in a little bowl with the cider vinegar – it will froth up. Stir this into the batter as quickly as you can, then pour into the tins, spreading evenly.

* Bake for about 30 minutes or until a skewer into the centre comes out clean. Leave to cool in the tins for 10 minutes, then turn out on to a wire rack to cool completely. The cakes may be a bit green on the outside but don't worry it's only the crust – the insides will be blue.

* Once the cakes are cool, make the frosting. Beat the butter until smooth. Add the cream cheese and mix until combined, then sift in the icing sugar and beat until light and fluffy. Cover the top of one cake with a layer of frosting then cover with the other cake. Using a palette knife, cover the top and sides of the whole cake with a thin layer of frosting (the 'crumb coat', see Tip on page 30). Leave to chill in the fridge for about an hour, until firm and set. Remove from the fridge then cover with the remaining frosting.

Wild Forest Gateau

JULIE GILBERT

Cream, kirsch and luscious cherries combine to make this a 'wildly' indulgent cake, with plenty of fun to be had making cheeky little marzipan beetles, bugs and other forest creatures to decorate the top.

SERVES 8–12

240g butter, softened
240g caster sugar
4 large eggs
190g self-raising flour
1 tsp vanilla extract
50g cocoa powder
1–2 tbsp milk

Filling:

1 x 400g jar pitted cherries
1 tbsp granulated sugar
1 tbsp cornflour
3 tbsp kirsch or sloe gin
300ml double cream

Icing:

200g icing sugar
1 tbsp cocoa powder
a few Oreo biscuits,
   crushed to fine crumbs

Decorative Forest Creatures:

250g ready-to-roll white
   sugarpaste or marzipan
a selection of food colourings
your imagination!

* Preheat the oven to 180°C/fan 160°C/gas mark 4. Grease and line two 20cm round sandwich tins.

* Beat the butter and sugar using a wooden spoon or electric mixer until light and fluffy. Add the eggs one at a time, beating well after each addition, and adding a tablespoon of flour with the final egg to help prevent curdling. Stir in the vanilla extract, then fold in the remaining flour and cocoa powder. Add enough milk to reach a soft dropping consistency.

* Divide the mixture between the tins, spreading it evenly. Bake for around 25 minutes, until the cakes are risen and a skewer inserted into the centre comes out clean. Leave to cool in the tins for a few minutes before turning out on to a wire rack to cool completely.

* While the cakes are cooling make the wild forest creatures. Knead your choice of food colouring into portions of the sugarpaste or marzipan and shape into little animals – real or imagined. Leave for a couple of hours to dry slightly, if you have time.

* To make the filling, heat the cherries and their juice with the sugar. In a small bowl, mix the cornflour with a tablespoon or two of water to make a smooth paste. Stir it into the cherry mixture, bring to the boil and simmer briefly until the mixture has thickened. Stir in one tablespoon of the kirsch. Set aside to cool.

* To assemble, place the bottom layer of cake on a plate and brush with the remaining kirsch. Spoon over the cherry mix then whip the double cream and spread over the cherries. Place the second layer of cake on top.

* In a bowl, mix together the icing sugar and cocoa powder. Add boiling water a tablespoon at a time until it is a pouring consistency. Pour the icing over the cake and guide it with a spoon until the top of the cake is covered. Allow the icing to drip down the sides of the cake. Sprinkle the crushed Oreos on to the icing, then place the forest creatures on the cake while the icing is still wet, to help them stick.

Neapolitan Cake

JINI MULUKUTLA

This attractive three-tone cake was inspired by the much-loved Neapolitan ice cream flavour. It's made by baking coloured strips of sponge side by side in the same tin. Don't worry if your lines turn out a bit wonky – the triple-colour sponge is impressive regardless!

SERVES 12

240g butter, softened
240g caster sugar
4 large eggs
240g self-raising flour
1 tbsp cocoa powder
1 tsp vanilla extract
pink gel food colouring

Decoration:
300g good-quality dark
  chocolate (min. 70%
  cocoa solids), broken up

* Preheat the oven to 190°C/fan 170°C/gas mark 5. Grease and line a deep 900g loaf tin measuring about 22 x 13cm on the base.

* Beat the butter and sugar using a wooden spoon or electric mixer until light and fluffy. Add the eggs one at a time, beating well after each addition, and adding a tablespoon of the flour with the final egg to help prevent curdling. Sift in the remaining flour and fold in gently.

* Divide the mixture equally between three bowls, either by eye or by weighing the mixture in each bowl. Stir the cocoa powder into one batch, the vanilla into the next and a little pink food colouring into the third.

* Place the cocoa batter in a line along the length of the prepared tin. Add the vanilla in a line next to it and finally add the pink batter. Bake for 30–40 minutes, until a skewer inserted into the centre comes out clean. Leave in the tin for about 10 minutes, then turn out on to a wire rack to cool completely.

* To decorate the cake, place the chocolate in a bowl. Melt it either in a microwave, stirring at 30-second intervals, or in a heatproof bowl set over a pan of gently simmering water. Stir until smooth, then let it cool slightly so it is not quite so runny.

* Place the cake on a large sheet of baking paper and spoon the dark chocolate all over the top and sides to give a smooth coating. Leave to set and then trim off the excess chocolate.

Oreo Rosette Cake

HELEN COSTELLO

This eye-catching cake was originally created for an American-themed cake club event, paying homage to the world-famous cookie. The rosette frosting may look tricky, but in fact it's very easy to achieve using a piping bag with a star-shaped nozzle. If you're cookie-mad, why not use even more irresistible Oreos to decorate your plate or cake stand?

SERVES 12–16

225g butter, softened

600g caster sugar

7 egg whites

450g self-raising flour

1 tbsp vanilla extract or the scraped seeds of 1 vanilla pod

355ml milk

1 x 154g pack Oreo cookies, roughly crushed (some chunks are fine)

Vanilla Frosting:

225g butter, softened

1 tsp vanilla extract

110ml milk

800g icing sugar

TIP

For the ultimate finish and sheen, sprinkle your piped rosettes with edible metallic lustre dust.

* Preheat the oven to 190°C/fan 170°C/gas mark 5. Grease and line two 20cm round, springform cake tins.

* In a large bowl, beat the butter and sugar using a wooden spoon or electric mixer until light and fluffy. Add the egg whites one at a time, beating well after each addition, and adding a tablespoon of the flour with the final egg to help prevent curdling. Add the vanilla, then add the remaining flour and the milk alternately. Stir in the Oreos. Divide the mixture between the tins, spreading it evenly.

* Bake for 50 minutes or until a skewer inserted into the centre comes out clean. Leave to cool in the tins for 10 minutes, then turn out on to a wire rack to cool completely.

* Make the frosting. Whisk the butter and vanilla until smooth, then beat in the milk and icing sugar alternately in three or four batches until well mixed and the frosting is stiff enough to pipe. Using a palette knife, coat the top and sides of the cake with a thin layer of the frosting then spoon the rest into a piping bag fitted with a star nozzle.

* Using a disposable piping bag and a large closed star nozzle (such as a Wilton 2D), start in the centre of the cake and pipe circles of frosting that will miraculously look like roses. Pipe as many of these rosettes around your cake as possible, filling in any gaps with dots of frosting.

* To finish, you can either tie a ribbon around the bottom of the cake to hide any unfinished edges, or arrange more Oreo cookies around the edge of your plate as shown in the photo.

Rainbow Cake

LYNN HILL

Get your colours right and you'll have a wow-factor cake that only reveals its stunning secret once you cut the first slice! I highly recommend using concentrated gel colour for best results, which can be bought online and from bigger supermarkets. Add just a tiny amount at a time until the correct shade is achieved. If you don't own enough cake tins, you can easily bake the sponge layers in batches, as they cook quite quickly.

SERVES 16

350g butter, softened
350g golden caster sugar
6 eggs
350g self-raising flour
1 tbsp vanilla paste or vanilla extract
5 different food colouring gels or pastes (not liquid)
coloured Smarties, to decorate (optional)

Filling:

100g butter, softened
150g full-fat cream cheese
1 tsp vanilla paste
50g icing sugar

Icing:

5 tbsp apricot jam, warmed and sieved
750g ready-to-roll white sugarpaste
icing sugar, to roll out

* Preheat the oven to 190°C/fan 170°C/gas mark 5. Grease and line five 18cm round sandwich tins.

* Beat the butter and sugar using a wooden spoon or electric mixer until light and fluffy. Add the eggs one at a time, beating well after each addition, and add a tablespoon of the flour with the final egg to prevent curdling. Add the vanilla, then gradually fold in the remaining flour until combined.

* Divide the mixture between five small bowls and add a different colour to each bowl a few drops at a time, using enough colouring to make the colour stand out. Mix until the colour is even. Transfer each coloured mixture to a separate tin, spreading it evenly. Bake for 12–15 minutes, until a skewer inserted into the centre comes out clean. Leave to cool in the tins completely.

* To make the filling, beat the butter until smooth. Add the cream cheese and vanilla paste and mix until combined, then sift in the icing sugar and beat until light and fluffy.

* To assemble, place the first layer of sponge on a firm stand or plate, spread with a quarter of the filling, then sandwich together with the second sponge. Repeat the process with the remaining layers.

* Brush the top and sides of the cake with the warmed, sieved apricot jam. Dust a surface with icing sugar and roll out the sugarpaste. Turn it frequently and use lots of icing sugar, rolling it until it is around 3–4mm thick and wide enough to cover the whole cake. Then pick it up over a rolling pin and carefully drape it over the cake. Press it gently down the sides of the cake, smoothing out any bumps, then cut off any excess icing. Carefully brush away any excess sugar using a pastry brush.

* Decorate with coloured Smarties, sticking them on with apricot jam or buttercream. This cake will keep in an airtight container for three days.

Cake Wrecks

Even with the most careful planning, sometimes good cakes go wrong. But rest assured, most cake disasters can be rescued in one way or another! Here are some of our best tips for saving the day.

CAKE HOLLOWS

A cake that has sunk or fallen in the middle is often the result of opening the oven door too soon and then banging it shut. The sudden drop in temperature (or even the loud noise) can cause uncooked batter to sink like a stone and even the patron saint of cakes would not be able to raise it back up. But never fear, if you do suffer a cake hollow, it can be disguised.

With a deep cake, slice horizontally through the centre, being careful to cut below – not through – the hollow. Now reverse the layers, placing the top (sunken) part onto your plate or cake stand first, with its hollow uppermost. Spread your chosen filling onto the sponge, adding extra in the middle to fill up the hollow. Once you have a level covering, top with the second sponge layer and then decorate as you wish – and no one will be any the wiser! If your cake isn't deep enough to slice into layers, leave in one piece and either frost thickly or fill the hollow with a mound of fresh berries and cream and make it a feature!

To avoid cake hollows in the first place, always wait until at least three-quarters of the baking time has passed before you even think about opening the oven. Once it's safe to open the door and test your cake, if you find that it's not yet fully cooked, be very careful to close the door gently and allow the cake to bake for a further 5–10 minutes before testing again.

DOMED CAKES

A domed cake is extremely simple to fix. Simply slice off the domed top and turn the cake upside-down, then decorate as intended. The offcuts can be frozen to use in a trifle.

UNEVEN RISING

A number of things can cause this, but generally it's best not to have too many things baking in the oven simultaneously, as this can result in an uneven temperature. Also try to avoid baking your cake nearest to where the heat is generated – position the tin in the centre of the middle shelf, where the temperature is most even. While the cake is baking, check through the glass to see if it appears to be rising more on one side than the other. If so, wait until three-quarters of the baking time has passed, then quickly open the oven door and rotate the tin. If your cake still ends up with an uneven surface, cut away any raised parts then either turn it upside-down or disguise any uneven surfaces using frosting or glacé icing (see page 248).

BURNT OR DARK CAKES

Don't panic – in most instances, it is probably only the edges and top that are burnt. So cut off the offending pieces with a sharp knife and, if necessary, turn the cake upside-down to hide any irregular edges. Then fill and frost or decorate as required and remember that sifted icing sugar will cover a multitude of sins!

Once you've rescued your cake, take stock and try to determine why it burnt in the first place so that you can prevent it happening again in the future. Were you engrossed by the TV or busy on the phone when you should have been checking the cake? Did you use a timer? Is your oven set to the correct temperature? If unsure of your setting, invest in an oven thermometer.

A great preventative measure for burnt or overly dark cakes is to cover the top with a sheet of baking parchment or foil, either for the whole cooking time or just for the last 10–15 minutes when the top has started to turn a lovely golden colour, but the middle is still not quite cooked through.

OVERCOOKED OR DRY SPONGE

This is an easy fix! Just soak the sponge with your favourite syrup or liqueur to make it moist and delicious. Do this by poking holes in the sponge with a skewer, then pouring or brushing on the liquid so that it permeates the cake. Alternatively, slice through the middle and fill the cake with a delicious jam. To avoid a dry cake, test the sponge with a skewer about three-quarters into the baking time – if it comes out dry and batter-free, remove the cake from the oven and allow to cool.

SOGGY UNCOOKED MIDDLES

To avoid a cake with a soggy middle, never open the oven door until at least three-quarters of the baking time has passed. And even when it is safe to open the door, never remove the cake completely from the oven to have a closer look, or you risk the temperature dropping too much for the baking to properly finish. Always keep your oven gloves and testing skewer close by, so that when you open the door to test the cake, you can do so very rapidly, allowing only the smallest amount of heat to escape from the oven. If the cake is still raw when tested and the skewer emerges with batter or wet crumbs on it, continue to cook your cake for 5- or 10-minute intervals depending on how loose or wet the centre is.

If it's too late and you only discover your cake is raw some time after you've removed it from the oven, don't be tempted to reheat the oven and put it back in. Instead, leave the cake to cool completely, then find a tin the same size as the soggy middle section, place over the offending area and press down like a cutter to carefully remove the uncooked portion. (Throw away all the raw batter as it's not suitable for eating, especially if it contains eggs.) Drizzle glacé icing (see page 248) over the remaining sponge and people will think you've deliberately made your cake in a ring-shaped tin.

CAKES THAT WON'T TURN OUT

If your cake sticks to the tin when you attempt to turn it out, leaving you with large broken pieces of sponge, mix up some buttercream or frosting and use it to stick the offending bits back together. Then cover the whole cake with frosting or a layer of ready-made sugarpaste to hide the joins. If it still looks a bit wonky or uneven, allow the first layer of covering to set, then add a second layer to improve the finish.

To avoid clingy cake in the first place, always grease and line at least the base of your cake tin, then also grease the sides. That way, the only parts at any risk of sticking are the sides, which you can release by running a round-bladed knife around the tin before turning out. Light sponge cakes should be left to cool for just a few minutes in the tin before turning out onto a plate, while cakes containing lots of fruit are best left in their tin to cool completely, else the soft warm fruit may cause the cake to stick and crumble.

DROPPED YOUR CAKE?

In this book you will read about a couple of real-life cake wrecks, when bakers dropped their cake tins en route to an event! If this happens, all is not lost. Small imperfections can easily be hidden with fresh fruits, berries, edible flowers or sugar decorations. If the damage is more extensive, such as a squashed or streaky cake, it's time to get creative! Remove any broken decorations and carefully scrape off streaky frosting or peel away bashed or cracked sugarpaste. Fix any broken pieces of sponge back in place with buttercream, and fill holes or build up missing edges using marzipan or sugarpaste. Then cover with a fresh layer of frosting, sugarpaste or even shop-bought ganache or marshmallow fluff, depending on what is available. Finally, add your choice of new decorations. Even if you're not in your kitchen when a cake wreck strikes, if you can get to a supermarket there are all manner of ready-made coverings, toppings and decorations you can use as a replacement. If it's worth baking, it's worth rescuing!

Icings and Frostings

GLACÉ OR WATER ICING

Quick and simple to make, this icing starts off runny and then sets to a nice shiny glaze. It can be tinted with food colouring if you wish. Or you can replace the water with lemon or lime juice for a zingy citrus-flavoured glacé icing.

Makes about 200ml (enough to glaze a 900g loaf or 18–20cm round cake)

200g icing sugar

warm water (about 2 tbsp)

food colouring liquid or paste (optional)

✳ Sift the icing sugar into a bowl. Add warm water a tablespoon at a time, mixing well after each, until you reach a consistency that is spreadable but not too runny (or the icing will drip off your cake). If you find you have added too much water, thicken the icing by mixing in some extra sifted icing sugar.

✳ Once you are happy with the consistency, add a few drops of food colouring, if using, and mix well. Drizzle over your cake and allow to set.

CREAM CHEESE FROSTING

I like cream cheese frosting thick and not too sweet, so I use a ratio of three parts cream cheese, two parts butter, one part icing sugar. The best results are with full-fat cream cheese, straight from the fridge, which helps maintain a thick consistency. This amount will fill and cover an 18–20cm round cake with two layers. For each additional layer, increase the ingredients by 25 per cent.

Makes about 600g (enough to fill and cover an 18–20cm round cake)

200g butter, softened

100g icing sugar, sifted

1 tsp vanilla paste or flavouring of your choice

300g full-fat cream cheese, straight from the fridge

✳ Beat the butter and icing sugar together until light and creamy, then add the vanilla paste or your choice of flavouring and mix well. Finally, beat in the cream cheese until well combined. If your frosting seems too thin, add a little extra sifted icing sugar. Fill and cover your cooled cake with the frosting.

BUTTERCREAM

This classic icing is simple to make and can be textured, swirled or piped into all sorts of lovely patterns. If you'd like flavoured buttercream, replace some of the milk with your choice of flavoured syrup or extract. You can also add food colouring if you wish. This amount will fill and cover an 18–20cm round cake with two layers. For each additional layer, increase the ingredients by 25 per cent.

Makes about 600g (enough to fill and cover an 18–20cm round cake)

200g butter, softened

400g icing sugar, sifted

2 tbsp milk

✳ Beat the butter until soft, then gradually add the icing sugar a little at a time until well combined and the mixture is light and creamy. Gradually mix in the milk (or your choice of colour/flavouring) until the buttercream reaches a spreadable consistency.

Index

Page numbers in bold denotes an illustration

Acknowledgements

I would like to begin by thanking all the CCC members who submitted their wonderful recipes – without them there would be no book. Also thanks to the many members and organisers who helped me build CCC into what it is today – a fabulous cakey phenomenon, and to Becs Rivett, who is on permanent standby for website fixes.

Many thanks to Stuart Cooper and Claire Potter of Metrostar Media, who saw the germ of an idea for a CCC cookbook even when the club had only been going for a few months, and who supported me throughout the process. My many trips to London for meetings meant the cold winter months were constantly filled with hope.

Thanks must go to everyone at Quercus: Jenny Heller and Ione Walder, you made this project a joy and helped keep my stress levels to a minimum. Thanks also to Bethan Ferguson, Lucy Ramsey and Mark Thwaite, and to the photography and design team – Caroline Harris, Anita Mangan, Emily Dennison and Abigail Read – for all their amazing work; I am so thrilled with the pictures, illustrations and design.

DRAWING OF LYNN HILL
BY ALEX GILMARTIN

And of course many thanks to Jane Middleton for all her support with the recipes and for making the cakes look so stunning, and to Imogen Fortes for the editing. This book has been such fun to put together.

Last but not least, thanks to my wonderful family David, Joanne and Richard. Without their constant love and support, I think I would have given up long ago.

Businesses and Blogs

Many of the Clandestine Cake Club Cookbook contributors run successful cake or food businesses, or write blogs about their baking and culinary adventures. You can find them online at:

Euan Greig	http://signorbiscotti.wordpress.com
Fionnuala Lawes	www.facebook.com/white.brownie.co
Gary Morton	http://exploitsofafoodnut.blogspot.co.uk
Gillian Tarry	www.patacake4tea.blogspot.com
Helen Costello	www.casacostello.com
Helen Jones	http://bakingaitch.wordpress.com
Jane Edgar	www.facebook.com/pages/ cakeaccasions/217413508272879
Jo Christy	www.secludedteaparty.com
Joanna Myers	www.the-greedy-pig.co.uk
Julia England	http://awannabefoodie.wordpress.com
Juliana Morris	http://goodgobble.blogspot.co.uk
Julie Gilbert	www.butcherbakerblog.com
Karen Burns-Booth	www.lavenderandlovage.com
Kay Cushnie	http://kayteascakes.wordpress.com
Lindsey Barrow	www.lancashire-food.blogspot.co.uk
Lisa Gair	http://theyummyyank.blogspot.co.uk
Marcus Bawdon	www.countrywoodsmoke.com
Mike Wallis	http://backwardslion.wordpress.com
Nelly Ritchie	www.nellyscupcakes.co.uk
Nicette Ammar	http://choclogblog.blogspot.co.uk
Paul Barker	www.cinnamonsquare.com
Pippa Sharp	www.pippas-pantry.co.uk
Rachel Baxter	www.comedinewithrach.blogspot.co.uk
Rachel McGrath	www.dollybakes.co.uk
Rachel White	www.honeypotcakes.com
Sally Harvey	www.lavenderattic.blogspot.co.uk
Sarah Ollington	www.yestercake.co.uk
Sharon Clarkson	http://humbugshouse.wordpress.com
Susan Aron	www.theartofpuddings.com
Vanessa Kimbell	www.juniperandrose.co.uk

Andrew Kite	http://catchkitey.tumblr.com
Annie Foley	www.anniescakestudio.co.uk
Becs Rivett	www.laythetable.com
Carla Gardiner	www.orangemartini.blogspot.co.uk
Carla Valentine	www.afternoon-tease.blogspot.co.uk
Carmela Hayes	www.carmelaskitchen.blogspot.co.uk
Catherine Pratt	www.lovedayteas.co.uk
Catriona Roscoe	www.cakesbycat.co.uk
Chris Holmes	www.mrcake.co.uk
Claire Melvin	www.claireshandmadecakes. wordpress.com

Quercus Editions Ltd
55 Baker Street
7th Floor, South Block
London
W1U 8EW

First published in 2013

Text copyright © Lynn Hill, 2013
Photographs © Emily Dennison, except page 6 and page 115 (bottom & top-right) © Jill Jennings
Illustrations © Abigail Read and Anita Mangan, except page 254 © Alex Gilmartin

The moral right of Lynn Hill to be identified as the author of this work has been asserted in accordance with the Copyright, Design and Patents Act, 1988.

All rights reserved. No part of this publication may be reproduced, stored in a retrieval system, or transmitted in any form or by any means, electronic, mechanical, photocopying, recording, or otherwise, without the prior permission in writing of the copyright owner and publisher.

Quercus Editions Ltd hereby exclude all liability to the extent permitted by law for any errors or omissions in this book and for any loss, damage or expense (whether direct or indirect) suffered by a third party relying on any information contained in this book. Every effort has been made to contact copyright holders. However, the publishers will be glad to rectify in future editions any inadvertent omissions brought to their attention.

Many thanks to Spring Hill, an imprint of How To Books Ltd, for their permission to reproduce the recipe for Cardamom, Rose & Rhubarb Cake (see page 91), originally published in *Prepped* by Vanessa Kimbell. Thanks also to Le Creuset for kindly loaning items for photography.

A catalogue record of this book is available from the British Library

ISBN 978 1 78206 004 8

Publishing Director: Jenny Heller
Project Editor: Ione Walder
Produced by: Harris + Wilson
Design (except back cover), illustrations and styling: Anita Mangan
Recipe testing and home economy: Jane Middleton
Copy-editing: Imogen Fortes

Printed and bound in China

10 9 8 7 6 5